T0100238

Linux System Administration for the 2020s

The Modern Sysadmin Leaving Behind the Culture of Build and Maintain

Kenneth Hitchcock

Apress®

Linux System Administration for the 2020s

Kenneth Hitchcock
Hampshire, UK

ISBN-13 (pbk): 978-1-4842-7983-0   ISBN-13 (electronic): 978-1-4842-7984-7
https://doi.org/10.1007/978-1-4842-7984-7

Copyright © 2022 by Kenneth Hitchcock

Managing Director, Apress Media LLC: Welmoed Spahr
Acquisitions Editor: Divya Modi
Development Editor: James Markham
Coordinating Editor: Divya Modi

Cover designed by eStudioCalamar

Cover image designed by Pixabay

Distributed to the book trade worldwide by Springer Science+Business Media New York, 1 New York Plaza, Suite 4600, New York, NY 10004-1562, USA. Phone 1-800-SPRINGER, fax (201) 348-4505, e-mail orders-ny@springer-sbm.com, or visit www.springeronline.com. Apress Media, LLC is a California LLC and the sole member (owner) is Springer Science + Business Media Finance Inc (SSBM Finance Inc). SSBM Finance Inc is a **Delaware** corporation.

For information on translations, please e-mail booktranslations@springernature.com; for reprint, paperback, or audio rights, please e-mail bookpermissions@springernature.com.

Apress titles may be purchased in bulk for academic, corporate, or promotional use. eBook versions and licenses are also available for most titles. For more information, reference our Print and eBook Bulk Sales web page at http://www.apress.com/bulk-sales.

Any source code or other supplementary material referenced by the author in this book is available to readers on GitHub via the book's product page, located at https://github.com/Apress/Linux-System-Administration-for-the-2020s. For more detailed information, please visit http://www.apress.com/source-code.

Printed on acid-free paper

To Arlene, Dad, and Mom, without your support and sacrifices, I would not have had the successes I had.

Table of Contents

About the Author

Kenneth Hitchcock is a principal consultant working for Red Hat, with over 20 years of experience in IT.

Ken has spent the last 11 years predominantly focused on Red Hat products, certificating himself as a Red Hat Architect along the way. The last decade has been paramount in Ken's understanding of how large Linux estates should be managed, and in the spirit of openness, he was inspired to share his knowledge and experiences in this book.

Originally from Durban, South Africa, Ken now lives in the south of England, where he hopes to not only continue to inspire all he meets but also to continue improving himself and the industry he works in.

About the Technical Reviewer

 **Zeeshan Shamim** has been an IT professional in various capacities from management to DevOps for the past 15 odd years. He has worked in roles ranging from support to DevOps/sysadmin in various organizations ranging from big telecom firms to financial banks and is a proponent of open source technologies.

Acknowledgments

This book is based on all the experience and training I received over the years, all of which started while working for Justin Garlick and Alasdair Mackenzie. Thank you for all the opportunities to learn and for giving me the foundation to get started in the open source world.

My eventual move to Red Hat opened opportunities to work with larger teams and allowed me to learn so much from so many great influential people in the various Red Hat teams. I am grateful for the guidance and friendship from Dan Hawker, Will McDonald, Vic Gabrie, Martin Sumner, Chris Brown, Paulo Menon, Zeeshan Shamim, and so many others I have not named who are from a truly special group of people that are always willing to help and make working at Red Hat so special. Thank you all for showing what it means to be open.

Introduction

This book is divided into four main parts with each designed to expand from the previous. More subjects are introduced as you go along; some may require further reading, and others are explained. At the end of the book, you will be left either feeling happy that you are doing things the right way or have a thousand ideas on how to improve.

Part 1

If you are reading this book with existing Linux knowledge, use Part 1 as a refresher or an opportunity to see things from a different perspective. It is entirely possible there is something you may not know or have possibly forgotten.

For the reader new to Linux, this is not a book to teach you all the foundational skills either or bring you to the same level as readers with years of experience; that will require more effort on your part. It will, however, give you the keywords and subjects you will need to explore further on your own.

Anyone who has ever been exposed to something new will understand the statement "you don't know what you don't know." Part 1 is there to give you the breadcrumbs to these unknowns; further chapters will give you a bit more. The value in Part 1 will come from the structure it gives; it will show you what to learn and where to focus to build a solid foundation.

The advanced users with many years of experience will most likely breeze through the first chapters and not gain anything new. All I can offer you is a different perspective on how I believe a solid Linux knowledge foundation can be laid.

Each of us comes from different backgrounds; we have different views on how things should be done and how we have always done them. Take Part 1 as either a refresher or a stepping stone to a greater understanding of the Linux and open source world.

Part 2

Part 2 will explore how to improve ways of working with Linux systems and hopefully give you a few shortcuts along the way. It contains much of my experience as a consultant from the last ten years and will contain some interesting views on what I have experienced a little more recently. The ultimate goal of this part is to bring you up to speed with the latest estate management trends and tools. Everyone who is reading this book should gain some benefit from what I am sharing with you.

It will start with new tooling and the new ways of working most organizations have started to adopt. Using these new tools, we will delve into estate management and how Linux systems have and should be provisioned. We will look into backing up and restoring platforms with a good understanding of the disaster recovery options available today. We will visit good and bad practices people commonly do and how to avoid them. We will then discuss best practices for running an efficient environment.

Like we discussed community and enterprise Linux distros in Chapter 1, we will discuss community and enterprise estate management tools. We will look at how these tools can be leveraged to build a solution that can be truly inspirational.

With good statement management, there needs to be a high degree of automation; in Chapter 5, we will explore in-depth automation concepts and practices to achieve higher productivity than what it was like to build systems ten years ago.

Finally, we will discuss different aspects of containerization, when is the right time and what should and should not be containerized.

Part 3

Day two operations are the most important aspects of keeping your Linux estate running. These are the nuts and bolts of tailoring your Linux estate to your organization's needs. Part 3 is going to be focusing on some of the most important day two configurations needed for a Linux system to be supported by your organizations.

Chapters leading up to Part 3 were not heavily focused on how to use these tools but more focused around what they were for and what you could spend your time looking into further.

In Part 3, however, we are going to focus on a bit more of the traditional Linux system administration day two operations. We will be looking at monitoring, logging, security, and how to plan system maintenance. Some of the tooling you may already be using, and some might not be what you have seen before. These chapters will explore what I have seen in the industry over the last decade and discuss some interesting new ways of working.

Part 4

The goal of Part 4 is to help you to understand how a problem should be seen and analyzed before taking any action, allowing for effective troubleshooting instead of guessing where the issues could be. Part 4 will give you a solid theoretical foundation to use when taking on difficult problems.

When a problem does go beyond our understanding or we just don't have the time to spend days trying to find the root cause, we need to ask others for help. Learning the correct ways on how to ask for help will save frustration when the community does not respond as you would have liked.

Finally, we will briefly delve into a few advanced administration tools that can be used to give you more information about your system.

PART I

Laying the Foundation

Before delving into advanced or intermediate topics around managing large or smaller Linux estates, it is very important that we establish the required baseline skills to fully appreciate this book. This is the main purpose of Part 1.

CHAPTER 1

Linux at a Glance

Where did Linux come from? Where is Linux going? Why should you not be afraid of using Linux?

These are important questions to anyone new to Linux or anyone who is looking to understand more about this amazing operating system. Linux has and continues to change the world; the opportunities Linux has already brought are astounding, but what it still has to offer is what truly excites me. Together with open source communities, Linux will continue to evolve, grow, and encourage innovation from millions of developers creating new projects across the globe. With the open collaborative nature of the open source world, we will be capable of anything. No problem can be too big.

During this first chapter, we take a look at the differences between community and enterprise Linux distributions. We will discuss why enterprise Linux is preferred by some and why community distributions are preferred by others. We will look at the different approaches some distributions have taken in how the operating system should be managed and understand why variations of distributions have spawned. Finally, I hope to help you understand the possible reasons why someone would use community or enterprise Linux distributions.

© Kenneth Hitchcock 2022
K. Hitchcock, *Linux System Administration for the 2020s*,
https://doi.org/10.1007/978-1-4842-7984-7_1

Brief Unix to Linux History

Long before Linux was even thought of, the world had Unix. Unix very much like Linux was created out of necessity.

Multics, a time-sharing operating system built by a few organizations, namely, GE, MIT, AT&T, and Bell, was not the success all had hoped it would be. Ken Thompson, Dennis Ritchie, and his colleagues walked away from the Multics project and started working on what we know today as the Unix operating system. During the 1970s, various changes and improvements were made that eventually led to Unix being taken more seriously. New compilers were added like C, which incidentally became the catalyst for new versions of Unix to be written with it.

One big sticking point for early Unix was around legal restrictions. Bell Labs was not able to sell Unix as a product unfortunately. This, however, did not stop Unix source code from miraculously making it out to the open world. It was rumored that Ken Thompson, who had many requests for the operating system code, finally relinquished and sent media with the Unix code to whoever requested it, often with a note "Love Ken." This "open" approach would of course catch on in later years, but more of that in a bit.

As with any new software development on a new project, there will always be different developers with different ideas on how things should be done. Unix development was no different, so naturally standards were nonexistent. The different development ideas and directions in the various Unix platforms were most prevalent during the 1980s when the three major variations of Unix came into existence. They were System V, BSD, and Xenix. In the 1990s, common sense finally prevailed, and COSE (Common Open Software Environment) was formed to set the standards of the Unix operating system. With these new standards in place, the Unix operating system went from strength to strength. Unix was being worked on as a global effort and no longer by individuals.

The beginning of Linux is not too different from Unix. Unlike how Unix was a fork of Multics, Linux is Unix reinvented from the ground up.

In the early 1990s, a Finnish student at the University of Helsinki named Linus Torvalds became fed up with the operating system choices available. Linus wanted to use Unix, but unfortunately or fortunately, depending on how you see it, Unix was far too expensive for a student. Left with only one choice, Linus started to build his kernel "Just for fun"[1] from scratch.

Around the same time as Linus was writing the Linux kernel, an American software developer by the name of Richard Stallman along with the FSF[2] were developing their own operating system called GNU. Linus and Richard Stallman along with the FSF were ultimately working toward the same goal, though from different ends. Linus built the kernel, and Richard with the FSF was building the utilities. The combination of these utilities and the kernel led to the creation of the first Linux operating system, "GNU/Linux."

Open Source

Open source does not mean "free." The fact that the software has no cost does not mean the software has no value; it means the source code is open and not locked away in a proprietary vault somewhere.

If the software has no cost, then what's the point, right? How can someone make money from it?

This is where companies like SUSE, Canonical, and Red Hat make their money. They sell subscriptions for the support of their distributions but don't actually sell the software. You can use Red Hat Enterprise Linux, for example, without a subscription, and you can update the operating system from community repositories with no problem. You can't, however, ask Red Hat to support you. For that, you need to pay.

---

[1] Just for fun is the name of the book written by Linus Torvalds
[2] Free Software Foundation

Linux Is Everywhere

Almost everything we use today from smartphones to laptop computers or the kiosk terminals we buy our movie tickets on at the cinema all share one thing in common: they all use Linux. Well, almost everything. I still see the odd Windows "BSOD" when I walk through the London underground. My point is, we use Linux or see it almost on a daily basis without knowing it. Linux is often used in train stations and airports for advertising boards, but did you realize the entertainment systems used on your flights are often Linux driven too? Maybe not the best example if you spent an eight-hour flight with no entertainment.

Linux systems like these are easier to develop and improve, and as the communities who maintain them are constantly working on bug fixes or new projects, this kind of development model drives innovation and constantly encourages investment from larger organizations to develop new ideas.

Hardware vendors are also beginning to understand why open source is better and are constantly looking into ways to make use of open source tooling. This cannot be stressed enough in the mobile or cell phone market.

In 2013, the Android market had 75% of the market share; today, that number is still around 72%. That is still an extraordinarily large percentage of the global smartphone market. Over five billion people use smartphones. That is, about two thirds of the planet's population use a mobile device. 72% of those devices use Android. This means that almost half of the world's population is using Linux right now.

Smart TVs, tablets, home automation devices, and IoT devices are not to be excluded either. Open source software has enabled these platforms and gadgets to grow increasingly more popular. Companies like Google, Amazon, and Philips are a few that have released really good products for simple home automation. People who are least technical today now have the ability to configure their home to allow lights to come on by schedule or motion.

It still seems like something from a sci-fi film when I see that a kettle can be set to boil water in the morning before even getting out of bed. If that doesn't interest you, imagine a smart device with a robotic arm controlled by a virtual chef that can be commanded to cook your dinner from a menu.

It is not just the innovation in our homes that is impressive, it is the automation that is going to change the world that excites me. I recently saw new automation tooling to manage a vegetable garden. The software used can detect and command a robotic system to remove weeds, water the vegetables, and spray pesticide.

These innovative devices and ideas have deep roots in open source and Linux. The availability of hundreds if not hundreds of thousands of developers and hobbyists has shown that collaboration far outperforms any proprietary software company development efforts.

These examples I mentioned are small scale now, but imagine at full scale; imagine hundreds of acres of farmland being automated to grow food or automated restaurants with robotic chefs that can cook anything you can select off a menu. Yes, there is always the human factor that could face the brunt of this innovation, and there too is an answer for that. By automating and innovating ourselves out of jobs, we are building systems and platforms to feed and clothe us. Just like our technology is evolving, so must we. Where the farmer toiled in the field, they now can spend the time enhancing the machine learning that drives the automation. The farmer now can spend more time with their family or innovating better farming techniques.

By following open source practices and giving back to the community, farmers can expand and feed more people. Building community projects and sharing with the planet only increases the ability for the eradication of starvation. It's these innovations that make the future bright and open new doors.

These ideas allow us to tackle difficult world problems and do what we as intelligent sentient beings should do. Improve the world we live in, not destroy it.

Community Linux Distributions

As the name implies, community Linux distributions, or "distros" as they are better known, are developed and supported by the community for the community.

This is great, but what does the term "community" actually mean?

Community

The "community" is a name generally given to a collective of people who do not work for a single organization to develop a product. Well, I suppose that is not entirely true. Some organizations like Red Hat sponsor communities to develop and work on community products to act as their upstream variants. These communities do prefer to focus more on the term "project" than "product."

Upstream

Another word thrown around in the open source world is "upstream." "Upstream" is a term used to describe what an enterprise product is based on. This doesn't mean the enterprise product is a direct copy of the upstream product either. The upstream is considered more of the "bleeding edge" or innovation breeding ground, typically used to prove and test new product features before being pushed into enterprise products.

If a product sponsor, like Red Hat, likes one of the upstream features, they take the code from the community and work the new feature into the enterprise equivalent. These features are then tested and reworked to ensure they are enterprise grade before releasing new versions to customers.

It is worth mentioning that the enterprise products often have different names than their "upstream" equivalents. Take the example of Fedora Linux. Fedora is considered the upstream for Red Hat Enterprise Linux or RHEL.

Community Contributors

For a community to exist or provide a product, the community needs contributors. Community contributors are typically software developers, hobbyists, or people who enjoy building and developing projects in their spare time. These contributors dedicate their spare time giving back code for anyone to use. For them, it's all about getting their work out to as many people as possible and sharing.

Note   One other thing to note is that giving back to the community doesn't only mean writing code. Being part of a community could be anything, provided you can contribute to the project or community in a meaningful way. It could be a monetary donation or giving up some of your time to host a meetup. Anything that can help grow the project will have value.

Common Distributions

At the time of writing, there were around 600 Linux distros available, give or take a few. Many are forks of more well-known distros, and some are forks of forks of forks.

As mentioned a few times already, open source is all about being open and having code available for anyone to use. This is why it's possible for anyone to create a new distro; in fact, there are distros that help you create distros.

One thing all distros have in common is the Linux kernel. So it all still comes down to what Linus is releasing. You are welcome to try to create your own kernel; I'm sure many have tried, but sometimes it is best to not try to reinvent the wheel, especially if it is still working well enough. There may come a time when the kernel needs to be reengineered, but till then we will trust in Linus.

The kernel is one of a few things that is the same across most if not all Linux distros. Differences that do exist between Linux distros are around package management systems. Linux distros like Red Hat Enterprise Linux, Fedora, and CentOS/Rocky use the RPM-based package management system. Distros like Debian and Ubuntu use their deb-based package management system.

Another less-known packaging system that seemed to be getting a bit of traction is Pacman. Pacman is currently being used by the gaming distro SteamOS and Manjaro.

With all the distros available, it's important to know where each distro came from and what that distro was built for. As mentioned earlier, Fedora is regarded as the "upstream" for Red Hat Enterprise Linux, but this is not what it was initially intended for. Fedora was first released in 2002 by Warren Togami as an undergraduate project. The goal of the project was for Fedora to act as a repository for third-party products to be developed and tested on a non-Red Hat platform.

Other distros have been built purely for security, like Kali Linux built and configured for penetration testing. A distro like Puppy Linux was built to be a cutdown distro to allow users to run a "lighter" Linux on older slower hardware.

As a small taste to that mindmap of all the Linux distros available, the following is a small part of the distro family tree for RPM-based distros. This table does not take into account the forks of forks of forks that have happened from these.

RHEL/CentOS	Fedora	openSUSE	Mandrake
Asianux	Berry Linux	SUSE Linux Enterprise	Mandriva
ClearOS	BLAG Linux	Desktop	Linux
Fermi Linux LTS	EnGarde Secure	SUSE Linux Enterprise	Mageia
Miracle Linux	Linux	Server	ROSA Linux
Oracle Linux	Fuduntu	SUSE Studio	OpenMandriva
Red Flag Linux	Hanthana	GeckoLinux	Unity Linux
Rocks Cluster	Korora		
Distribution	Linpus Linux		
Rocky Linux	Linux XP		
Scientific Linux	MeeGo		
Amazon Linux 2	Russian Fedora		
	Remix		
	Trustix		
	Yellow Dog Linux		

Which Distribution Is Best for You

With all the distros available, for any new users the choice of which distro to choose could be a daunting task and may just end up scaring the potential new user away.

So how do you go about choosing the correct distro for you?

To make the decision on what distro is best for you, you need to ask yourself the right questions.

The following are a few questions that I like to consider when choosing a distro. I'm sure there are many more good ones, but these I think are a good start:

1. Is this going to be used to expand my knowledge or just replace what operating system I currently have?

2. Do I need to use any Windows products?

3. Will I be gaming on the platform?

4. How much control do I want from the platform?

5. How much do I want preinstalled and configured?

Before Committing

The best approach for any new user moving to Linux, who may not be familiar with Linux or open source tools for that matter, is to do a staged approach. Start by changing to open source tools on your current operating system. Change to using a Firefox browser or use Thunderbird for email. Find open source alternatives to products you currently use and get familiar with them. Once familiar with the new tools, then switching to Linux will seem less of a culture shock.

Tip   Make a list of all the tools you use and search the Internet for open source alternatives, then switch one by one. Try different products if some are not right for you or spin up a virtual machine with a distro you think works for you and test your alternative tools there.

The Three Linux Distro Categories

In my personal opinion, there are three categories of Linux distros you can use:

- The simpler "out-of-the-box" distros with everything working from day one

- The "almost out-of-the-box" options which have almost everything you need but require some tweaks

- The "challenge accepted" distros, where everything from the install to configuration takes time, patience, learning, and experience

Option One: Out-of-the-Box Distros

Easy to Understand

For new users of Linux, you will want to look at something that is simple to install and easy to understand, something that just works well "out of the box." Distributions like Ubuntu, Zorin OS, and Elementary OS are simple to use. All in some respects have similarities to Windows which could make the switch a bit easier for users from a predominantly Windows background.

Installation Should Not Require a Degree

The other important aspect to finding the best distro for first-time Linux users is that the distro needs to be easy and uncomplicated to install. There are not many hardware vendors selling laptops or desktops with Linux preinstalled, so it's important the user can install the distro without getting frustrated. The install should be as simple as booting from a DVD or USB and clicking install. A simple install will help when the inevitable reinstall is required. No new user is going to want to install something overly complicated involving in-depth configuration steps. A simple, next, next, finish install will do.

Try Ubuntu

Ubuntu, for example, is a good choice for someone new to Linux. The install is simple, the methods of creating install media are not overly complex, and there are enough one-minute google searches to find answers on how to create bootable media. The installation itself does not require much thought; defaults work quite well and will leave the user with a suitable installation.

Ubuntu configuration could involve a small learning curve for the brand-new user. Ubuntu does however have a nice "apps store" to find almost anything.

Applications like Wine and Lutris work quite well on Ubuntu, which means gaming is possible with less frustration. Lutris itself is a very useful tool in that it wraps configuration required for games to run on Linux quite nicely. The scripts are easily found in Lutris and can be added with relative ease.

Walk Before Running

My advice for any new user is to start with Ubuntu or something very similar. Get familiar with how Linux works in general. Learn about systemd, and understand how firewalls are configured.

Get familiar with installing drivers for hardware not included in the kernel, like graphics cards. Spend time on discussion boards learning how to figure things out for yourself.

Push yourself and learn how to configure your Linux distro as a web server or a plex server for your home as a fun starter project.

Option Two: The Almost Out-of-the-Box Distros

Choosing a distro that requires a bit more understanding is a good way to take the next step in your Linux knowledge. These distros are recommended for the user that has been using Linux for a short while already and who may wish to start experimenting with more complex configuration, possibly to try to incorporate work elements and understand new features for enterprise products, and maybe even to move your work environment to Linux.

Try Fedora, openSUSE, or Debian

If computer gaming is not important and the use of Windows products is not required, you can consider either Fedora, openSUSE, or Debian. All are good options to consider. They all require "tweaking" to make them right for you, but if you are not too bothered, you can use them as is.

Personally, I prefer using Fedora. It's the "upstream" for RHEL which helps me for my day job, and it's what I have been using for the past ten years. As for the default desktop, I really don't like Gnome or KDE, so I have installed Cinnamon.

Fedora, however, is not great for gaming or installing Windows products. Drivers for graphics cards are not brilliant and can be a challenge to install sometimes. Not impossible but seems a bit more work than Ubuntu, for example.

Installing third-party tools will also require new repositories installed and sometimes need to be "massaged" to work. Online instructions are not always clear, which means you need to think a bit more about what the problem is. In most cases, it's fairly straightforward and can be figured out with enough patience.

Option Three: The "Challenge Accepted" Distros

If a challenge is something you prefer, then the more "difficult" distributions might be something to consider. Using these more challenging distros will involve experience and understanding on how to configure the platform, often with limited help from online resources.

Using these distros may get you referred to the dreaded RTFM[3] when asking for help online. It is not that the community for these distros can be difficult, they are predominately made up of super smart people with not much time to spare, who really are not interested in helping people who do not want to help themselves.

Note In a later chapter, I will discuss how to ask technical questions. Something all technical people need to learn to avoid irritating people when asking technical questions.

With Great Power …

These "challenge accepted" distros provide more "power" to the user (not that other distros don't have the ability). They provide more options and opportunities for users to break the platform without too much thought. These distros require taking care when running commands or configuration changes. Running commands without knowing the consequences will more than likely lead to a rebuild of the system.

Try Arch Linux or Gentoo

If you are still interested in the challenge, then distros like Arch Linux and Gentoo are ones to consider. They are known to be more difficult to install and have a sharp learning curve.

---

[3]Read the Freaking Manual

These distros should be used when you are comfortable working out issues on your own and don't need too much guidance. You should be well versed in finding meaningful errors and understand where to increase verbosity when needed.

Compiling from code and rebuilding kernel modules should not be something you have not done before either. In some cases, getting applications or drivers to work will involve these kinds of tasks. Distros like Arch Linux and Gentoo should be left for the die-hard fans who wish to set themselves a challenge, so do not take them lightly if you are predispositioned to frustration.

Enterprise Linux Distributions

Red Hat, SUSE, and Canonical (Ubuntu) have built their companies around the paid subscription model. As the software and code are open source, these companies cannot sell you the software. Instead, they sell you support and enterprise-grade product updates. As a user, you can use the products as you wish, provided you do not breach the license agreements, that is, claiming the code is yours and turning it into proprietary code.

Note   Read the license agreements to make sure you are not breaching any of the rules if you are unsure.

Where enterprise products really pay for themselves is around the product updates these companies provide. These updates are vital for companies that require enterprise support, like banks. Banks require a high degree of security. They rely on companies like Red Hat to provide up-to-date security updates for vulnerabilities when they are made public.

If banks did not use enterprise products and opted to use community-based products, they would need to wait for the community to fix a vulnerability when it is reported. This can sometimes take a couple hours or a couple days if not weeks.

If the vulnerability was a particularly bad one, it could cost the bank more than any software subscription ever would. It could even spell the end for some organizations if they were to be breached because of a vulnerability waiting to be fixed by the community.

Enterprise Linux companies may make money from the software they support, but do not think for a minute they do not help the communities to help develop their products. Enterprise Linux companies have become extremely important to the communities from which they get most of their "upstream" products. Red Hat as an example not only uses "upstream" projects like Fedora for RHEL but also has many, many other "upstream" projects they support. It is this support that grows the products and promotes adoption throughout the whole industry.

Red Hat

Red Hat has a large portfolio of enterprise products from Red Hat Enterprise Linux all the way through to the OpenShift container platform they use as their hybrid cloud solution.

Red Hat has been developing solutions since their start in 1993 and hasn't stopped trying to release the next best enterprise product. Red Hat is constantly setting the trend in enterprise open source solutions; if Red Hat has not actively been developing new products, they have been acquiring companies that have. An example of this is the acquisition of StackRox recently.

Red Hat builds their business around three main product categories that drive their business and customer adoption.

Red Hat Enterprise Linux

RHEL is the boat that started Red Hat on their journey across the turbulent sea of migrating customer workloads to Linux. It's what keeps the company ahead of the competition and continues to be what made Red Hat one of the big names in the Linux world. Over the years, Red Hat has become more than just a Linux provider and now boasts a large portfolio of products from infrastructure products through to cloud solutions. Red Hat has come a long way from when they were selling CDs for RHEL.

Automation

With the acquisition of Ansible in October 2015, Red Hat strengthened their offerings to the market with one of the best automation products yet. Red Hat not only made Ansible enterprise grade but also took the previously proprietary Ansible Platform (Ansible Tower) and open sourced it. The community version of Ansible Platform is called AWX.

Ansible continues to grow in popularity and continues to be one of the most actively developed automation products in the community. There are new modules being developed constantly to improve the product almost on a daily basis.

Hybrid Cloud

The cloud is something all of us now know about. It is nothing new; most organizations are actively looking at cloud options if they have not already moved or are planning the move for future roadmaps. Red Hat is no different.

Red Hat over the years has become very good at finding the next big thing. This was the case with the acquisition of Makara in 2010. What made Makara so special was because of their PaaS (Platform as a Service) solution they were developing. In May 2011, OpenShift was announced from this acquisition, and in 2012 OpenShift was open sourced.

OpenShift is the premier hybrid cloud solution at Red Hat; OpenShift provides an orchestration layer for containers, which allows customers to migrate workloads from on-premise to cloud and vice versa. Red Hat is investing massively into OpenShift, which is constantly evolving and has become the number one choice for most organizations when choosing a container orchestration tool.

OpenShift is one of the key products IBM targeted for their Open Hybrid Cloud solution when they acquired Red Hat.

Canonical

Canonical was founded in the UK by Mark Shuttleworth in 2004. Canonical is better known for their community Linux distro called Ubuntu. Very much like Red Hat, Canonical offers paid support subscriptions for their products. Ubuntu, however, is not like Red Hat Enterprise Linux and Fedora. There is only the community Ubuntu product. Canonical offers support and break/fix where it can but does not actually have its own distro like Red Hat does.

Canonical like Red Hat has a portfolio consisting of more than just Linux support. Canonical offers products in the following categories.

Linux Support

The first and obvious part of Canonical's business is around their support for Ubuntu. As discussed before, Ubuntu is only developed by the community and supported by Canonical for a price.

Cloud

Canonical offers support for Kubernetes, which is a container orchestration product similar to OpenShift. For their private cloud solution, Canonical supports and helps install OpenStack. Both products provide cloud capabilities for Canonical.

Internet of Things

One area Canonical is different from both Red Hat and SUSE is their support around IoT devices and embedded Ubuntu. More companies are looking for a Linux distro for their "smart" devices and appliances. Canonical has an edge in this market as one of the only enterprise Linux companies to provide this level of support.

SUSE

SUSE, the third and by no means last enterprise Linux company, currently has a slightly wider portfolio than Canonical, but not quite that of their closest competitor, Red Hat. SUSE, like Red Hat, has their own enterprise Linux distro. The community version of SUSE Enterprise Linux is called openSUSE. The enterprise version of SUSE has support subscriptions from SUSE Linux Enterprise Desktop through to SUSE Enterprise Linux for IBM Power.

SUSE as mentioned has a slightly wider portfolio than Canonical. Currently, SUSE has two product categories driving their business, which may be an unfair oversimplification of their products.

Server and Desktop

The first product category is the one that SUSE has built their business on: their enterprise Linux distribution. SUSE has many Linux variations from Desktop through to IBM Power versions. All have different subscriptions that can be purchased, and most if not all are driven by the "upstream" openSUSE product.

SUSE remains a strong competitor to Red Hat Enterprise Linux in the server operating system market. It is not uncommon to find data centers with both SUSE and RHEL.

Cloud, Storage, and Management

Alongside their enterprise Linux offerings, SUSE has a few other products they sell subscriptions for. SUSE has their own enterprise storage solution based on Ceph; this is the same as what Red Hat does for their enterprise storage solution. Ceph is also used in OpenStack and OpenShift, which means customers could effectively have a SUSE Ceph cluster and combine it with Red Hat solutions if they wanted to.

For cloud platforms, in particular around hybrid cloud and container orchestration, the recently acquired Rancher (acquired in December 2020) provides competition to Red Hat's OpenShift.

SUSE, Red Hat, and Canonical all provide OpenStack for private cloud capabilities. All companies support the platform and provide professional services to deploy and configure OpenStack.

To manage SUSE Enterprise Linux, SUSE supports a product called SUSE Manager. SUSE Manager is based on Spacewalk and SaltStack, very similar to the first Red Hat Satellite product which too was based on Spacewalk and Puppet.

Community vs. Enterprise

What are the reasons to use a community product vs. a supported product? Why use a paid-for solution when you can get the same or similar for free?

The preceding questions have already been answered if you understood the differences between enterprise and community. Using examples always clears things up for me personally, so let's take a bank, for example, in particular, a bank that processes credit/debit card transactions. There is a strong possibility that these kinds of banks are governed by PCI DSS type compliance and regulatory requirements, often requiring stringent controls around the security and platform vulnerability, particularly on systems where card data will be stored. One very important

PCI DSS compliance requirement is that the customer's platform uses software that has been thoroughly tested and passed intensive security scrutiny, preferably by reputable companies that have been approved by various compliance auditors and have been accredited for their security. For this one main very important reason, you will always find banks using enterprise products and not community products.

A bank is one good use case for enterprise Linux, but what about someone who does not need regulatory compliance? What about a charity as another example? Most charities do not process credit/debit card data. Charities also tend to have quite small IT footprints, in that they mostly work out of cloud platforms or have limited physical hardware on-premise. All these points make charities an ideal prospect for community products. The charity would need employees who know how to find answers and resolve simple enough issues. Maybe someone reading this book, for example. As community products don't have support numbers to call or support desks to raise cases with, these charities would need their employees to do the hard work instead. Remember that this would only be for unforeseen issues and would be relatively rare. Proper test, preprod, and production platforms tested and verified should reduce risk and ensure enough stability.

Another use case for community products are technical people like ourselves. Not all of us are fortunate enough to have access to corporate accounts with unlimited subscriptions and need to have alternatives for our own personal projects. Building our home labs or personal web servers could be ideal for community products. We are more than happy to work things out, and if worse came to worse, we could rebuild and restore from backup. Ok stop laughing. Some of us actually back up our home labs (I don't).

The most important thing to remember about choosing a community product over enterprise is knowing you are left to resolve the inevitable vulnerability. Companies like Red Hat, Canonical, and SUSE are prepared for security vulnerabilities. They have dedicated staff who find zero-day vulnerabilities and fix them before they become public. Communities tend to be reactive and are always behind the curve when releasing security patches. Something large organizations like banks prefer not to have. You and me, we can turn our labs off if we are concerned about a security issue. Banks do not have that privilege.

Knowledge Check

For the best use of this book, you are expected to know the basics of Linux system administration. This would include things like

- Basic Linux system commands

- Basic Linux system configuration including how to manage storage devices and how to add new users

- Basic Linux security concepts

If you are not familiar with these things, it is advisable to do some further reading before continuing with this book.

This book, however, is hopefully written in a way that you will still benefit from its contents, but it will serve you better if you have a solid Linux foundation.

Summary

In this chapter, the following subjects were introduced:

- The very brief history of Unix and Linux

- How Linux is everywhere, in your smartphone, TV, and flight entertainment systems

- What community Linux distributions are and who develops them

- How to decide what distro is best for you

- What enterprise Linux options are available and what companies provide them

- The main differences between community Linux and enterprise Linux

PART II

Strengthening Core Skills

Now that Part 1 has been completed and expressed where you should be as a Linux system administrator, Part 2 will focus on building new skills in areas you may not have had exposure to yet.

CHAPTER 2

New Tools to Improve the Administrative Experience

Now that the basics have been covered in Chapter 1, we can start looking at new ways to improve what you are currently doing. This chapter will focus on how you as a Linux system administrator should be working, what tools you should consider using, and how these tools can improve your efficiency.

This chapter will start by looking at task management, how to create background tasks, and how to work in a way that you can leave tasks running when you need to leave for the day. We will then go on to start looking at the basics of Ansible. With Ansible, we will only discuss the very basics to get you started. Later in the book, we will dig further into automation. For this chapter, it is only important to get you up to speed with the beginnings of Ansible if you have never used it before. Then to finish the chapter off, we will look at what consoles can be used to make Linux configuration easier.

By the end of this chapter, you will not only know how to manage tasks slightly better but will also have some foundational Ansible knowledge to start automating. You will also have been shown alternative methods to configure Linux other than the traditional command-line options.

© Kenneth Hitchcock 2022
K. Hitchcock, *Linux System Administration for the 2020s*,
https://doi.org/10.1007/978-1-4842-7984-7_2

Task Management

The Linux operating system is in essence a series of files and processes working together to assist the user in completing computational requests. These processes need to be managed occasionally. As a user of Linux, it is recommended to understand how processes can be started, stopped, and, when it is required, killed, sometimes forcibly.

Starting a Process

Starting a process can be done in a number of ways; the most common one you will use is done by starting a service. Starting an apache web service, for example, usually involves starting the httpd service. This service spawns a few httpd processes depending on your configuration. A service however is really nothing more than a script or a set of commands that call a binary followed by parameters. When looking at your process, the parameters are often listed after it.

Starting the apache web server as mentioned requires a service command. With most Linux distros, this will be a systemctl command:

```
# systemctl start httpd
```

To check if the service has started, you can replace the start parameter with the status parameter, or you can check what processes are running that match the name httpd:

```
# ps -ef | grep httpd
```

The output should look something like

```
root      150274        1  0 22:48 ?        00:00:00 /usr/sbin/
                                                     httpd -DFOREGROUND
apache    150275   150274  0 22:48 ?        00:00:00 /usr/sbin/
                                                     httpd -DFOREGROUND
```

```
apache     150277   150274   0 22:48 ?          00:00:00 /usr/sbin/
                                                 httpd -DFOREGROUND
apache     150278   150274   0 22:48 ?          00:00:00 /usr/sbin/
                                                 httpd -DFOREGROUND
apache     150279   150274   0 22:48 ?          00:00:00 /usr/sbin/
                                                 httpd -DFOREGROUND
root       150506   108621   0 22:48 pts/2      00:00:00 grep
                                                 --color=auto httpd
```

Task Visualization Tooling

Viewing what processes are running is important to understanding what your system is doing, or what is causing your system to act up. Viewing processes can be done in a few ways. You can use utilities installed by default, or you can use the ps command and search for your process. On Fedora, I did not have any issues installing any of the packages mentioned as follows.

Top

Top is installed by default on almost every Linux distro I have ever used. Executing the command "top" should give a similar output to the following:

```
# top
top - 21:51:30 up 35 days, 22:34,  1 user,  load average: 4.80,
5.38, 3.13
Tasks: 423 total,   1 running, 421 sleeping,   0 stopped,
1 zombie
%Cpu(s):  8.8 us,  6.9 sy,  0.0 ni, 81.9 id,  0.0 wa,  1.8 hi,
0.6 si,  0.0 st
```

```
MiB Mem :  23679.7 total,   1453.4 free,   11263.9 used,
10962.5 buff/cache
MiB Swap:   8192.0 total,   8190.8 free,       1.2 used.
10835.9 avail Mem

   PID USER       PR  NI    VIRT    RES    SHR S  %CPU
%MEM     TIME+ COMMAND
  3219 ken        20   0   17.3g 237396 144936 S  16.9
1.0 106:56.90 chrome
  1033 root      -51   0       0      0      0 D  10.6
0.0  21:58.24 irq/136-rmi4_sm
129564 ken        20   0   20.6g 323744 123548 S   9.9
1.3  14:31.80 chrome
 29109 ken        20   0 4450712 196656 105148 S   9.3
0.8  34:17.92 cinnamon
  2021 ken        20   0 1051020 103268  62488 S   8.6
0.4  37:08.53 Xorg
108567 ken        20   0  754204  42076  30860 S   3.3
0.2   0:08.86 gnome-terminal-
  3171 ken        20   0   16.9g 489020 192036 S   1.7
2.0  66:08.40 chrome
  3220 ken        20   0   16.5g 131584  92976 S   1.0
0.5  28:09.36 chrome
151128 root       20   0  236260   5568   4376 R   1.0
0.0   0:00.15 top
150042 root       20   0       0      0      0 I   0.7
0.0   0:08.40 kworker/1:2-events
    14 root       20   0       0      0      0 I   0.3
0.0   1:09.19 rcu_sched
  1140 dbus       20   0   13396   9064   2644 S   0.3
0.0   0:20.92 dbus-broker
```

```
  3177 ken         20   0    7768    4120    3304 S   0.3
0.0    2:19.38 cgroupify
  3532 ken         20   0  20.7g 404148 123592 S   0.3
1.7   12:04.38 chrome
 49421 systemd+  20   0   17712    8712    7832 S   0.3
0.0    1:25.22 systemd-oomd
 83705 ken         20   0  20.6g 119640  79348 S   0.3
0.5    0:11.45 chrome
 97202 ken         20   0  20.6g 147012  97388 S   0.3
0.6    0:13.16 chrome
```

Alternatives to Top

There are a few alternatives to "top" if you want to try something different (Table 2-1). Personally, I have tried and used a few but always default to top, mostly as the systems I work on are not my own. If you have not tried the alternatives to top in Table 2-1 before, I recommend you install and see for yourself if they add any benefit to your way of working.

Table 2-1. *Alternatives to top*

Top Alternative	Description
atop	Interactive tool to show load and other useful information on your system
htop	Very similar to top, except you can use your mouse to scroll vertically or horizontally
glances	A monitoring utility designed to show as much information as possible on one screen. Useful if you want to view information about sensors
bpytop	Very nice custom utility with a nice text-based interface. This utility will require you to download the source and compile

nmon

nmon is another very useful tool to help diagnose issues on your system. It is typically not installed by default but can be installed on most platforms. nmon has a very clear method of showing CPU, memory, disk, and kernel, to name a few. It's definitely a tool I would recommend using.

Killing Processes

Occasionally, there may be a need to kill a process; this could be for anything from a hung thread to a process with a memory leak. Before you kill this process, always ask yourself if killing the process is the best way of terminating your process. I do understand that sometimes there is no other option, and the task must be killed. However, never start by forcefully killing a process. Always start by trying to use service commands like systemctl or similar. Some applications or utilities have their own custom tools that can also be used. Read the official documentation or man pages to see if there is a recommended method.

I have experienced in the past that some system administrators do not always understand the implications of killing a process. I once worked with a system administrator who thought it was a good idea to forcibly kill a PostgreSQL database process as his main method of stopping the database service. This not only scared me but showed me the system administrator really did not understand the knock-on effect he could be inflicting on himself if he persisted with this behavior. As a consultant working with him at the time, I explained why this was a horrible idea and then stepped him through proper procedure.

If you ever do have to kill a process, always try to follow the following steps:

1. Get the process ID by using a process viewing tool like "top" or "ps."

2. Attempt to politely kill the process using the kill
    command without a parameter. This will default
    to using the "TERM" signal, which effectively tells
    the process it is going to be killed, and if it has any
    handlers, they would then attempt to run cleanup
    tasks, before terminating.

    ```
    kill <process id>
    ```

3. If the "nice" approach did not work, you can apply
    the sledgehammer approach. This will forcibly kill
    the process, and the terminate event cannot be
    caught, meaning the process will not be able to run
    any cleanup jobs.

    ```
    kill -9 <process id>
    ```

There are numerous other signal options for the kill command, each
used for different situations. The "kill -l" command will give you a list of
all signals that can be used.

Zombie Processes

Let's first understand what a zombie process is. A zombie process is when
a process has been killed, and its memory descriptor EXIT_ZOMBIE has
not been cleared by its parent process. This is normally done when the
parent process executes the wait() system call to read the dead processes'
exit status and any other information. After the wait() has completed, the
EXIT_ZOMBIE memory descriptor is cleared. When this is not done, it is
usually down to either the parent process misbehaving or bad coding.

I once heard a very simplistic explanation for killing a zombie process.
"You cannot kill something that is already dead."

It makes perfect sense if you think about what a zombie process actually is. It is nothing more than a memory descriptor that has not been cleared. No amount of kill commands will clear it. You would need to find the memory descriptor in memory and clear it yourself, which we all know, no one is going to bother to do it. Clearing the zombie process will involve a reboot unfortunately.

Finding the underlying cause for the zombie process will involve looking at the application whose process died. Was the code poorly written? Did the parent process die first? In my experience, this is usually due to system instability by having another process or application pulling the rug from under the process.

Utilities like "top" have a dedicated area to show zombie processes. If you see zombie processes appearing, there is a larger problem with your system that needs to be resolved. Chapter 11, we will discuss how you go about diagnosing issues and finding solutions.

Background Tasks

Services when started create background running tasks, largely because no system administrator wants to have an active session running all the time and the fact that it would just be plain silly to do so.

Background tasks can be viewed by looking at tools like top or running the ps command, but what do you need to do to send a task to the background? What happens when you start a long-running process and need to do other tasks? You could open a new window or console and run the task there. However, a better approach would be to send the current task to the background. The following are the basic steps to send a current running task to the background:

1. Press the "CTRL + Z" keys.

   - This tells the Linux operating system to suspend the current task and returns the user back to the shell.

2. Once back to the shell, execute the command "bg".

    •   This command sends the current suspended task to
        the background and resumes running.

If you want to bring the background task back to the foreground, you simply execute the "fg" command.

Running Time-Consuming Tasks

As a system administrator, you will often need to run scripts or tasks that take a long time to execute. Sometimes, running these long tasks can get quite frustrating if you are running them on your laptop and you want to leave for the day. Fortunately, you don't have to wait till your task finishes if you use the right tools.

There are a couple tools you can use to help you with time-consuming tasks and allow you to get back to enjoying your life away from work.

Screen

A highly popular multitasking tool used by many is "screen." Most Linux system administrators will have used or at least know about "screen" and will most likely already know the basics, but for those new to Linux, "screen" is a tool that allows the user to create sessions that run as background processes. The user can disconnect and reconnect to a session as they wish, which means a long-running script or process can be left running in a screen session while the user disconnects and goes home. In the past, the task or process would have been tied to the user's session, and once the user disconnected, the tasks would be killed.

Screen is found in most distros and can be installed quite simply by attempting to install a package named "screen."

To use the screen in a very basic way, all you need to know are the commands listed in Table 2-2.

Table 2-2. *How to use "screen"*

Command	Description
screen	Starts a new screen session
ctrl + a followed by d	Disconnects you from the running screen session but leaves the session running
screen -list	Lists all the screen sessions
screen -r <session name>	Reconnects to the running screen session

Note   It should be noted that some distros have stopped shipping "screen" in some of their new versions, but the package is still available in community repositories.

Tmux

With less availability of "screen," a new tool being used is "tmux." "tmux" like "screen" allows a user to disconnect and reconnect to a session except that "tmux" has quite a rich set of features. I personally now use "tmux" on all my Linux platforms. The commands have become muscle memory, and I am often feeling lost when I work on a system without "tmux." It sounds strange to say that, but as a Linux system administrator, we are often asked to troubleshoot issues, and this involves being able to multitask. We may need a window running a watch command with another window tailing a log. Flipping between these windows can be chaotic when you have tons of applications running. So to avoid this, using "tmux" allows me to create a split screen and new windows within tmux. I am able to flip between sessions, and best of all, I don't have to leave the comfort of the command line.

Very much like "screen," there are a few basic commands you need to know to start using "tmux." From there, you can expand your understanding by reading the man pages or the help.

Table 2-3 list some of the common commands you will use in your day to day activities.

Table 2-3. *How to use "tmux"*

Command	Description
tmux	Starts a new tmux session
ctrl + b + d	Disconnects you from the running session
tmux list-sessions	Lists all the tmux sessions
ctrl + b + %	Splits screen vertically
ctrl + b + "	Splits screen horizontally
ctrl + b + w	Shows a window in tmux with all tmux sessions for you to switch to
ctrl + b + arrow keys	Allows you to resize windows

Ansible Introduction

The role of a Linux system administration has evolved over the last decade into more of an automation engineer role. More system administrators are writing automation code than ever before. The traditional Linux system administration role is slowly becoming less important than it used to be. You may be reading this book because either you are trying to learn what you should be doing to stay relevant in the fast-moving Linux world or you are new to Linux and want to learn how to start.

The answer to both questions is automation and in particular Ansible. Standard tasks like system patching or system configuration are all automated these days and require less manual intervention. Linux system administrators not only still need to understand how to configure Linux but also now need to know how to automate these configurations. Ansible is one of the most popular automation tools available today and would greatly benefit you in your career growth if you started to become more familiar with it. There is a dedicated chapter on automation a bit later on in this book where we will look a bit deeper into practices around automation. For this section, we just look briefly at the very basics of Ansible.

Installing Ansible

Installing Ansible is fortunately not too complex compared to some other tools you can use for automation. This really makes good sense as one of the driving factors to use Ansible is the easier learning curve to use it.

Ansible can be installed in two ways.

Package Management

The first and simplest way to install Ansible is through your distros package management system like dnf or apt.

Simply trying to install the Ansible package will work on most community distros as they generally have Ansible available in their standard repositories. Enterprise distros like Red Hat Enterprise Linux, however, require separate subscriptions and access to different repositories. For those distros, ensure you follow their official documentation on how to enable the required repositories.

> **Note**   Installing Ansible through a package management system is the recommended approach as this not only installs the Ansible binary but also prepares your Linux system with all the other supporting Ansible configuration files, allowing you to work in the best possible configuration.

Pip

Another way to install Ansible is through the Python preferred installer program, or commonly known as pip. There are no subscriptions or different repositories required other than getting pip itself installed. Once pip is installed, Ansible can be installed via the pip install commands.

> **Note**   When installing through pip, always be sure to check the version of Python that pip will be installing into.

Configuring Ansible

The heart of Ansible is the YAML you write that executes a task. For this, there is very little that you need to configure. If you installed Ansible via a package management system like dnf or apt, you will have configuration files created for you. If you installed via pip or downloaded binaries, you will need to create configuration files yourself.

The Ansible configuration file is called ansible.cfg and can be used to customize Ansible within its limits. As an example, you can configure where plugins or inventory files are stored if you wish to configure a nonstandard environment.

Configuration files however do need to be stored in specific locations for Ansible to be able to read them if not told otherwise. There is also a hierarchy Ansible will follow in which files Ansible will read first.

You can create Ansible configuration files in the following locations. It is also in this order that Ansible will read the configuration files. If it does not find the first one, it will move on to the next. If Ansible finds no configuration files, it will assume defaults.

- ansible.cfg file in the current directory you are working in.

- .ansible.cfg in your user home directory.

- Create the /etc/ansible/ansible.cfg.

Ansible can also be told where to find the configuration file by setting the ANSIBLE_CONFIG environmental variable.

Note   When creating the Ansible configuration file in the user's home directory, it is vital that the file is called ".ansible.cfg" and not "ansible.cfg". If you do not start the file with the ".", it will be ignored.

Ansible Inventory

Before using Ansible, you need to know how to target systems that Ansible will execute commands or tasks on. In Ansible, we do this with the help of an inventory file. If Ansible is installed from a package management system, the default inventory file created is /etc/ansible/hosts. This file can be used as is, or you can edit your ansible.cfg to tell Ansible where the inventory file can be located. Another common method of specifying where Ansible can find an inventory file is done when executing the "ansible" or "ansible-playbook" commands with the "-i" parameter, followed by the path to the inventory file.

The basic layout of an Ansible inventory file consists of a group name in square brackets, followed by a list of systems that are part of a group. In the following example, two servers are part of the "webserver" group, and one is part of the "database" group:

```
[webserver]
servera
serverb

[database]
serverc
```

Running Ansible

The Ansible command-line tools are made up of a few binaries. The two commonly used ones are "ansible" and "ansible-playbook." The "ansible" command can be used to execute single ad hoc commands directly to a host, whereas the "ansible-playbook" command is used to execute playbooks which can contain many Ansible tasks. An example of an ad hoc Ansible command used to ping all hosts in your inventory file can be done as follows:

```
ansible all -m ping
```

To run a playbook, you can use something similar to the following:

```
ansible-playbook -i /path/to/inventory /path/to/playbook.yaml
```

Ansible is relatively straightforward to run and does not require any configuration to use it. To get familiar with Ansible, run a few ad hoc Ansible commands to start, then move on to creating your own playbooks.

Playbooks

Once you have graduated from running Ansible ad hoc commands, you will want to progress on to creating playbooks. Simply put, a playbook is a way of running multiple Ansible tasks one after another. The Ansible playbook needs to start by specifying a host or group that the tasks will execute on. A variable file or list of variables can also be added, but for a very simple playbook, this is not really required. The following is a basic example of a playbook:

```
---
- name: "Install webserver"
  host: webserver
  tasks:
    - name: "Install httpd"
      yum:
        name: "httpd"
        state: present
```

Roles

Playbooks can become quite complex, and often there are times when you will want to reuse code. This is where Ansible roles become useful. An Ansible role is a way of using Ansible to do a specific job. This could be as simple as installing a package or as complex as deploying an entire cloud platform. Typically, a well-written Ansible role should execute without issue, out of the box. A default variable should be configured, so if the user does not set anything, the role will still run. A good Ansible role should also include a README.md file with instructions on how to use the role. The role should also include metadata that can be used by Ansible Galaxy.

Role Directory Structure

A role directory structure should be similar to the following, but can also be simplified to just the task directory as a minimum. The full structure does include additional directories that are not always needed, like the vars directory or the templates directory:

```
[Role name]
 -> [tasks]
   --> main.yaml
 -> [defaults]
   --> main.yaml
 -> [handlers]
   --> main.yaml
 -> [meta]
   --> main.yaml
 -> [vars]
   --> main.yaml
```

Note   Ansible role names should typically start with "ansible-role-", then followed by what you want to call the role.

Generating Ansible Roles

Another binary that is installed as part of Ansible is the "ansible-galaxy" binary. This binary can be used to manage Ansible roles and collections. This includes the ability for an Ansible role skeleton to be generated. To create a basic role structure to start you on your journey of Ansible role development, run the following command:

```
# ansible-galaxy init <your role name>
```

Modules

Ansible modules are another important aspect of Ansible not many people understand. If an Ansible role can be seen as a toolbox, the Ansible modules can be considered the nuts and bolts.

In the "Playbooks" section a few pages back, there was a playbook example. In the example, I used the "yum" module to install the "httpd" package. This "yum" module is part of the standard Ansible collections and does not require any additional installation. The "yum" module in this example tells the system the play is being executed on ("webservers") to use the "yum" binary to install the "httpd" package.

Some modules are much more complex than the "yum" module and can be more complex to use. Fortunately, Ansible documentation is fairly good and offers a good explanation of all the parameters and options a module generally has. To view the documentation, you can either do a quick Internet search or use the command-line help for Ansible. An example can be to look at the help for the yum module:

```
# ansible-doc yum
```

Ansible modules are typically written with Python. They can technically be developed with any development language, provided the language used is capable of outputting JSON. Modules should perform a single task and must return the outcome of the task. It is also very important that the module be written to be idempotent.

Sharing Your Ansible

Sharing Ansible knowledge and code is what has been making Ansible probably the best automation tool available today. The community efforts in developing Ansible modules have been amazing with vendors from all corners contributing code to promote Ansible adoption. It's not only vendors but system users like ourselves who too have been creating Ansible modules for almost anything you can think of.

Note   Once you have become more familiar with Ansible, consider giving back your code to places like Ansible Galaxy.

Ansible Galaxy

Ansible Galaxy is an excellent way of sharing your Ansible with the world. This not only gets your name out for others to recognize but also adds to the ever-growing library of Ansible that can be used by everyone.

When confronted with the need to write a new Ansible role or module, always start by searching the Ansible Galaxy for anything you could use or at least start with.

Web Consoles

Linux system administration has traditionally consisted of logging into a system via ssh and running various command-line commands to configure the platform as required. This can still be done today, but with the growth of Linux. System configuration was always going to evolve to include easier-to-use methods to accommodate newer users to Linux while they were learning.

Cockpit

Anyone who has built and configured Linux servers will know very well that desktops tend to not be used much on server platforms. Most of the time, all that is required is ssh and whatever software is needed for the server to perform its function. For this reason, there needed to be an alternative to a desktop for quicker and easier graphical user interface configuration.

This is where Cockpit has become useful. Cockpit allows a Linux server to be accessed by a web console. In the web console, the user has the ability to configure storage, network, and various other configurations. The user can also open a terminal session to the system and run command-line commands.

Cockpit would normally be used on server platforms only but can be installed on any platform that supports using cockpit.

Installation

Very much like most software installations on Linux, it is recommended to install "cockpit" using your package management system. On Red Hat Enterprise Linux, this would be yum or dnf, and with Ubuntu you would use apt. The following is the installation for RHEL or Fedora:

```
# yum install cockpit -y
```

Configuration

Once installed, ensure that the "cockpit" service has been enabled and started:

```
# systemctl enable cockpit && systemctl start cockpit
```

Check that "cockpit" is running:

```
# systemctl status cockpit
# netstat -nap | grep LIST
```

Finally, ensure that if you have your firewall running, port 9090 has been opened for tcp traffic:

```
# firewall-cmd --list-all
```

Using Cockpit

Once installed and configured, you should be able to open a web browser and enter the hostname or IP address of your Linux system with port 9090:

https://<Hostname or IP>:9090

The web console should now open and ask for credentials. The username and password can be any local user, and if you know the root password, you can use that too.

Within "cockpit," you can configure your network interfaces, add storage via NFS or iSCSI, and view logs. There are a few nice features like the ability to join domains from the web console and view what applications are installed on your system. Most of the configuration is self-explanatory and simple enough to understand.

Limitations

One of the main limitations of Cockpit is that it is a web console of the running Linux server, which simply means the server has to be running and the "cockpit" service needs to be working. You cannot use "cockpit" to resolve boot issues and cannot use "cockpit" to install any virtual machines.

Alternatives to Cockpit

Where there is one project in the open source world, you can be positive there will be many more similar to it. This is exactly the same with Linux web console administration. While Cockpit is the common option to use and does provide quite nice features, it would be worth mentioning some alternatives that can be used.

Note   Due to the nature of Linux being open source, my recommendations and alternatives will be nonproprietary software and generally open source products. Even though there can be good proprietary options, they will be for you to find and read about.

Webmin

Very much like Cockpit, you are able to configure various configuration options like adding new users or starting and stopping services. The downside to Webmin is the slower product update release cycle. Where Cockpit aims to release versions every two weeks, Webmin can go long periods without updates. This can, however, also be seen as a good thing. Best advice would be to compare these products for yourself and see what works best for you.

Ajenti

Another really nice web console alternative to Cockpit is Ajenti. Very much like Webmin and Cockpit, Ajenti provides a clean and easy-to-use web console that allows the user to configure the Linux platform it is installed on. The same limitations are present in all of these web consoles and will only provide configuration for the system it is installed on.

Text Consoles

If web consoles are not for you, then text UI tools may be something more up your alley. Text consoles or "tui" tools provide quick configuration options for the user when they are not familiar with all the command-line parameters. A good example is configuring authentication on RHEL back in the day. In the early days of RHEL configuration, you would need to dig out the help and work out all the various parameters you would need to get your command to be successful. Running a text UI for authentication now gives you all the options that can be selected or deselected. You don't need to remember any parameters other than connection details. The configuration is quicker and simpler with less room for error. Something I would advise when under pressure.

Installing

There is not just one package to install for all tui consoles. Each application would need to provide its own "tui" if the standard "tui" packages are not installed.

Using the Linux system's package management system, try installing the "tui" by adding "-tui" at the end of the package name. An example of this could be trying to use the NetworkManager text UI. If the package is not installed, try installing the following:

```
# yum install nm-tui -y
```

Using

Text consoles are simple enough to use and are generally self-explanatory. Best way to get to know them is by starting to use them. I personally have been using the NetworkManager "tui" to configure network configuration, mostly because it is faster and I have to remember less.

Summary

In this chapter, you were introduced to the following:

- How tasks can be managed on a Linux system and how you can work with background tasks.

- Ansible basics and how quickly you can learn Ansible to become proficient in a matter of hours.

- The power that comes with web consoles to manage Linux platforms.

- That not everything has to be done with a long command and a million parameters. Text consoles can save time and effort.

CHAPTER 3

Estate Management

The last chapter discussed new tooling or ways of working, and this chapter will continue in the same vein. However, it will look at the bigger picture of your estate: what things you should be doing and what things you should be avoiding.

Not only during this chapter will we look at how Linux estates have been managed by people in the past and how this can be improved on, we will also delve into system building, system patching, and tooling you should be using or should consider using. With this, we will briefly discuss management software that can be used today. The main idea of this chapter is to introduce you to how you can change your ways of working to make your life easier when managing these large estates.

We not only will discuss technical aspects of Linux estate management but will also look into ways to conduct proper planning and how to avoid those awful midnight patching cycles requiring engineers to work out of hours. This chapter will explore ideas to streamline as much of the manual work that the traditional Linux system administration used to require. We will discuss how you can start cultural change within your organization and how you can start driving conversations to promote innovation and spend less time firefighting.

Toward the end of this chapter, we will discuss common bad practices Linux system administrators sometimes do. We will then end the chapter with some recommended good practices Linux system administrators should start doing if not already.

© Kenneth Hitchcock 2022
K. Hitchcock, *Linux System Administration for the 2020s*,
https://doi.org/10.1007/978-1-4842-7984-7_3

Outdated Ways of Working

In my experience as a Linux consultant over the last decade, I have met many amazing people. Some taught me new interesting things and in some cases new ways to do things. On the other side of the scale, I have met others that have frustrated me in their lack of progress or forward thinking. This is not to say they were not any good; in fact, most have been incredibly smart people who have just been stuck in situations where the organization they were working for has just not afforded them the opportunity to grow, learn, or try new things. My frustrations often did not just end with the individual but also extended to the offending organization. By not promoting growth and new innovative ways of working, the Linux system administrators I worked with became stagnant and bored, often ending up with them leaving the organization.

So with this in mind, here are a few examples of what I mean when I say "outdated ways of working."

Outdated Skills

More often than I would like, I meet Linux system administrators who are not constantly updating skills. Some of the individuals only have themselves to blame, and some unfortunately are not supported by the organization they work for. Examples of this include not being familiar with new changes and known issues in new releases of the products they administer, often due to lack of training. Other examples include not staying up to date with changes in the market and new trends being used for platform management. Other issues involve organizations not wanting Linux system administrators to introduce new technologies within their environments. This often means the Linux system administrators would need to experiment in home labs or sandbox environments, which some might not have access to. For whatever reason, the Linux sysadmins' skills become outdated and leave them stranded with the organization that refuses to support them.

Keeping Knowledge to Themselves

This one is the worst of the worst. I have come across people who kept others at arm's length when it came to work they did. The intention it seemed was to not show anyone else what they were doing so they could secure their job just a bit longer. These people tend to be very reluctant to have anyone else collaborate on any projects with them and tend to overengineer everything they do. This is not something I would recommend doing in today's working environments. The more you share, the more you learn; often, the previous point regarding outdated skills and this one go hand in hand. If you are guilty of doing this, my advice is to start learning as much as you can about emerging technologies and start working with others. This not only will improve what you are doing but will also open new avenues for you, maybe even with a different organization and possibly a larger salary.

Over Engineering

This brings me to something I think we all have been guilty of sometimes: making a project overly complex for the simple requirement it was required for. If I had a penny for every time I saw something that was just completely overengineered for simple tasks, I would be a wealthy man. Just take a step back and ask yourself, do I really need to add all this complexity into this script or into this piece of work? If the answer is no, then cut the excess and keep the task simple. Use the "KISS" acronym if you have been guilty of overengineering in the past. "Keep it simple silly."

Shell Scripting

We all have written our fair share of shell scripts, and, yes, sometimes it cannot be avoided, and for those situations you just have to grin and bear it. However, when possible, try to use newer automation tooling to manage your systems or execute the task you wanted to do. Management software can also be leveraged to manage systems without the use of shell scripts. Changing your approach to using alternatives to shell scripting will begin your transformation into larger estate management from a central location. Not to mention, less maintenance for you to do on old shell scripts.

New starters to your organization will also not need to hassle you to understand what your script does; you could just redirect them to read the official documentation on the management tool you are using.

Today, there are less and less good reasons to write shell scripts other than quick wrapper scripts or quick scripts to test something. Scripts should not be used for anything permanent and most definitely not for anything in production.

Snowflakes

Every snowflake that falls to earth is unique; at least this is what I have been told and read. This sometimes is how Linux estates have evolved. Linux system administrators have built systems where each one has become its own unique snowflake. Each Linux system in the estate becomes so different with its own unique configuration, not to mention overly complex that it becomes so bad that no one in the organization knows what the system does or how to rebuild it. These systems scare me more than anything. They require so much effort to work out what is required when they need to be rebuilt and become a liability if platforms need to be failed over to a disaster recovery site.

Tip   The first step to improving your estate management and reducing firefighting is to get rid of as many snowflakes as possible.

Reinventing the Wheel

The best for last, writing a script or a piece of software to do something that already exists within the operating system is an unforgivable act. Unless there is an extremely good reason, this should be avoided. Even when writing Ansible, always see if something does not already exist. It saves time and your company's money. Just don't do it.

Build Process

The Linux build process is normally something you think about or spend a fair bit of time doing when you are building or managing a medium to large estate. For the home hobbyist or individual user, you tend to not be too bothered with this process and tend to just build your system manually. In larger estates, it is not uncommon to be asked to build ten or a hundred systems for different reasons. Building these systems manually is not a good option anymore with how the industry is evolving.

The days of building systems that cannot be replaced are over. Systems are now being treated more like cloud instances. If it breaks, drop it and redeploy. This process makes sense as it saves time and energy. No need to try firefight the problem on the spot or even fix the root cause there and then. Just drop the system and redeploy. Most systems send logs externally, so troubleshooting and root cause analysis can continue later when production is up and running.

Twenty years ago, this way of thinking would have got you some interesting looks and if management heard could have got you escorted out the building. Fortunately, times have changed and today this way of thinking is encouraged.

To understand how to improve, we need to understand what we are doing wrong. For this, let us discuss different methods of deploying Linux systems, what makes them worthwhile doing, and what makes them something to avoid.

Manual Installation Methods

The first method to discuss is the good old manual deployment. This may be fine for the odd random system you wish to test or play with but definitely not something you want to do if you have a hundred systems to build. You will definitely not find favor with your employer if you spend a week doing something that should be done in 20–30 minutes.

With all the ways that systems can be built including the many different tools or management systems you can use to build them, building systems manually should not be one of them. However, as we are learning what to avoid, let's start from the beginning and get a good understanding of how this manual process should be done and look at the manual build methods that have been used to install Linux. Later in the chapter, we will discuss how these processes can be streamlined.

Boot Media Install

The simplest method is using boot media to do your deployment. This could be a DVD or USB device. The system is generally started from your install media, and once your system boots into your Linux installer, you typically run through the manual steps. Defaults can be selected as the simplest option but is not recommended if you are building anything other than a test system. Important things like disk partitioning and package installation could be customized for any system of importance. If you are building a system that will be used as a template, then careful attention should be made during this install. You really do not want to have a template configured incorrectly, especially if it will be used to deploy the entire estate later.

Network Install

Booting off your network through an NFS server is another method of deploying a Linux system manually. This would still require boot media where you will need to redirect the install to a network location. This install method would require an NFS system running with the install media exported and available for use. You would still need to run through the install manually, and you would still need to ensure you do not just select defaults if you are building a production system. This can be streamlined if you have a kickstart file but will require some further understanding of how kickstart files are written. Fortunately, we live in a world where information is available freely on the Internet. There are many examples of kickstart files and many forum questions and answers to get you started.

Templates

Even though there are ways of imaging physical machines, it won't be something you do very often. Virtual machines, however, are another story all together. As you are reading this as a Linux sysadmin, I'm assuming you already understand the process of creating a virtual machine from a template and have most likely done a few clones in the past. If not, the process is quite straightforward. A Linux system is generally created and installed manually on the virtualization platform. Once built and configured, the virtual machine is then converted to a virtual machine image or appliance, depending on the virtualization platform you are using. This image can be locked or converted into a template to avoid unwanted editing or configuration drift. From this template, new virtual machines can be created with the operating system installed and ready for customization.

Virtual Machine Images

If you do not want to build your own Linux image, another would be to download an image from the vendor you choose to use for your enterprise Linux estate. Companies like Red Hat have prebuilt images available for download for each version of their operating system released. These images can be imported and converted into templates; from there, you are able to build systems. The entire process can be automated to streamline the process even further.

Tip   Using the network installation is a good way to start automating your deployments. This could definitely improve your build process if you are still deploying manually. Foreman is a community product, so if you cannot use Red Hat Satellite or SUSE Manager, it definitely is an option worth looking into.

Automated Linux Installations

Now that manual installs have been covered, we need to start discussing how to streamline the process. The first step to reducing wasted time when building new systems is to automate as much as possible. This should include as much automation as possible to get your system "production" ready. There are two approaches you can use.

Method 1: Network Install

The first way of automating a Linux build would be to use a network install option. For that, there are a few things that need to be available.

PXE Server

For Linux systems to build from a network, you will need to have a system listening for build requests. This is known as a PXE boot server. This system effectively allows a "fresh" system to boot from its network adapter and prompt a user to select what they wish to deploy, that is, if you have multiple builds you use. Default options can also be configured for a system to automatically build without user intervention.

Typically, the network boot server would be something like a Red Hat Satellite server or a Foreman server. If you choose to use your own DHCP server, these systems do require the DHCP system to redirect the "Next Server" option to these systems once a network address has been allocated. Personally, I would recommend using the DHCP servers that come with Satellite or Foreman. It makes life a bit easier to manage and avoids having to get central DHCP systems configured. It also can reduce complexity with firewall configuration if the traffic needs to span firewalls. Satellite and Foreman can also be configured to listen on different network interfaces, allowing DHCP and DNS segregation if you are concerned about unwanted DHCP or DNS impact on your network.

Tip Red Hat Satellite and Foreman will be discussed more in depth in the next chapter.

Kickstart

Once a system has booted into the network installation, the PXE server would need to be configured to deliver the installation instructions. This is known as the kickstart file. Kickstart files are basically answer files for the Linux installer. These files can be used for network installations and for ISO or USB device installations.

A good kickstart file should be configured to deploy a basic installation of the Linux distro you are using. With the main focus being around disk layout and basic package installation, keeping a kickstart file simple will allow you to use the same kickstart file for a variety of different system types.

Method 2: Virtual Machine Templates

This method is mainly for building virtual machines. However, it may be possible for physical machines to be built from images with technologies similar to PlateSpin. For that, you would need to figure out the process before continuing here.

For the purposes of this section, we will only be referring to virtual machine building.

Hypervisor API

With the network installation option on the previous installation method, you required the use of a PXE boot system. Deploying Linux systems from templates, however, does not require the Linux operating system to be installed as that was already done in the template. What you will need is a method of speaking to the hypervisor that currently hosts the template for your deployment.

To speak to a hypervisor for system provisioning, there are a few options available:

- Ansible modules

- Puppet or similar

- Custom shell script

- Management systems like Satellite, Foreman, or SUSE Manager

With one of the preceding methods, you can automate the provisioning process for your hypervisor to create a virtual machine from a template. The template creation can also be automated to pull down images from the Internet if you want to streamline further.

Ansible Examples

For the preceding process, I personally recommend using Ansible. Ansible offers an easier learning curve and is the current market trend for automation. The Ansible modules are already available with Ansible, and additional modules can be added by installing the required Ansible collections. Other than the modules, there are more than enough examples available online to show you how to automate almost anything you can think of. In fact, if this is something you wish to pursue, have a look at my GitHub repositories for some basic examples on Ansible. One particular Ansible role I have been involved in developing over the last couple years is one called "ansible-role-cornerstone." This Ansible role helps the user build virtual machines in VMware and Libvirt and also allows the user to provision cloud instances in AWS and Azure.

```
https://github.com/kenhitchcock
```

Using Images

If the template deployment model is something you wish to pursue, it will be worth understanding which approach is best to use: using a golden image or using a catalog of images.

Golden Image

The "golden image" model involves one image or template created as the base starting point for all systems. This image would be the central source of truth that everything can be built with. Let's have a look at some reasons to use this approach vs. to not use it.

Use It

- One image to manage and maintain.

- No chance of image sprawl creating chaos.

- One source of truth. You know what is in it.

Don't Use It

- If your image is not 100% correct, you can end up with an estate of Linux systems that would need to be rebuilt.

- Cannot be used to quickly spin up systems to be used out of the box. Configuration would still be required.

- Minimal time saved with using a basic image.

Note   This is not an approach I would recommend anymore, largely due to the fact that there are much better ways of automating system builds today. This method was mostly used in the early days of Linux estate building.

Image Catalog

This catalog can be virtual machine templates, images, or kickstart files. All will have similar advantages and disadvantages.

If you decide to use a catalog of images or kickstart files, it is recommended that you keep a track of what the images are used for and how they can be used for variations. The following is a basic example:

- [Base Linux OS image]
    - [Web server image]
        - [Load balancer image]
        - [Reverse proxy image]
    - [Database server image]
        - [Mysql image]
        - [Postgresql image]

This method of managing your build process does seem like a good idea on the surface, but it is important to understand the additional work it can bring. Let's break this down into some advantages and disadvantages for comparison.

Advantages

- Catalog of prebuilt images or kickstart files that can be used to build systems quickly. Allowing a repeatable build every time.

- Systems can be almost 100% configured for use after deployment.

- Templates can be sealed to ensure no configuration drift occurs.

Disadvantages

- If you use templates for virtual machine cloning, the templates will need to be patched and could be forgotten.

- Image sprawl could happen, and you could end up with a hoard of templates no one knows what they are for.

- Multiple images will need to be patched and maintained by someone.

Build Process Flow

To improve the build process in any organization, we need to understand the flow. Once we have a good breakdown of the flow, we can see where things can be automated and where improvements can be made.

Basic Build Process

A rudimentary flow of a Linux system build would typically look something like Figure 3-1. Add the approval process before the request is done and factor in the checks for available resources, and you have a basic flow for getting a new Linux system built.

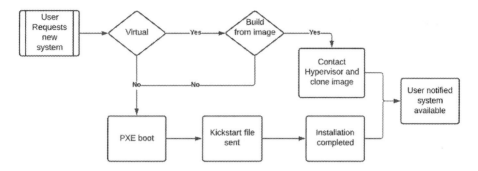

Figure 3-1. *Linux system build*

This solution is still used by many organizations today and has not changed much over the last decade other than the versions of the operating systems being installed.

What Can Be Improved

With this example of our basic build process, we have much scope for improvement and automation. Let's understand what can be done to improve this process.

Automate, Automate, Automate

It really goes without saying, automate every possible manual thing you do in your build process. This includes tasks outside of the installation or deployment. The allocation of network addressing, dns configuration are vital when trying to automate a full end-to-end system. Absolutely everything you would normally do manually must be automated.

Introduce a User Request Portal

By using a user request portal of some type, you remove the need for your engineers to be assigned basic build jobs. Not only should system builds be automated as mentioned previously, the process to request systems should also be streamlined.

Integration with Other Platforms

The user portal should be able to integrate with systems like change management platforms, where build requests can automatically be sent for approval. Once a job has been approved, the portal should have the ability to speak to an automation platform to kick off build jobs. Once the jobs are complete, the user should be notified.

Simplify Resource Requirements

Using "tee shirt sizes" for system build within the user portal will reduce complexity for end users. There will still be a requirement to determine what resource requirements would be needed for the user's build, but this can be done with documentation or notes during the user request process.

Use an Automation Platform

The use of an automation platform is highly recommended when trying to automate complete estate builds. The features provided often help make the process a bit easier, often giving guidance and tips along the way.

Some automation platforms like Red Hat Automation Platform could also be used by the user as a request portal to kick off approved builds. Some customization and user access control would be required but could be possible to a certain degree. Community versions of Red Hat Automation Platform can be used, but remember that there will be differences. An example would be the lack of directory services integration.

Alternative ideas and systems could involve anything from a Jenkins Pipeline through to customer scripts or applications. There are also higher-end paid-for products that can be used, but that will depend on your appetite for enterprise products.

Introduce Expiry Dates

For nonproduction or developer platforms that are only used for small jobs or tests, introduce methods of retiring them automatically. Give the user an option to extend if you want, but make sure unused systems expire and are deleted. This is not always possible but should be considered when you allow users to request new systems. Without something like this, you can quickly reach limits on hardware, or, worse, if you are using cloud platforms, you could incur massive costs.

Automated Build Process Flow

If all of the recommendations and more are adopted, your new build flow should not only reduce day-to-day build work. It will also allow complete estate rebuilds and improved recovery from disaster. The need to firefight systems that failed will be reduced as they could just be reprovisioned and be available for use within minutes or within the hour. With proper disaster recovery and failover, little to no downtime should exist. Figure 3-2 takes into account a few scenarios but should include much more around testing and system customization.

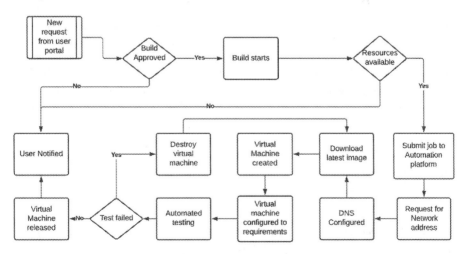

Figure 3-2. *Standard build process can be improved to eliminate manual configuration*

By improving your build process, more time can be spent on more exciting work, and it can improve innovation.

System Patching

System patching is one of the most important jobs a system administrator should be doing. Most companies or organizations that require accreditation can be fined or worse if systems are not patched regularly. For this reason, patching is planned and executed regularly with most organizations. This often means patching or updates need to be done out of hours and within certain maintenance windows, a painful task for the poor sysadmin assigned the job, especially when the work ends up being at 1 a.m. in the morning.

Let's first understand what the different update types are and then understand how patching and updates can be managed in a streamline manner to potentially reduce out of hours work.

Update Types

Linux updates for enterprise distributions are made available to customers who pay for subscriptions. Previously, we have gone over before, but to reiterate, these subscriptions are what divides enterprise from community. Enterprise Linux companies like Red Hat and SUSE will constantly be releasing updates. These updates come in two forms: package updates and errata.

Package Updates

Package updates make up the bulk of most system patching cycles. The updates tend to be new features or new versions of the installed package. Normally, during the update cycle, the package manager or package install files would make backups of any configuration files that may be impacted. However, never take it for granted that this will be done. I once came across an issue where a product was updated and overwrote the customizations made in the configuration file. My advice would be to always ensure you have backups in place before any update cycles are run.

Errata

Another update type commonly found with Linux updates is the errata update. Errata are the bug fixes and security updates. These make up probably the most important type of update you will need to install. It is in these errata you will receive the important security fixes when vulnerabilities are discovered in a package or file. These errata must be applied to any production environment as soon as possible.

Note   As the sysadmin of your Linux estate, ensure that you are getting all alert emails with errata releases. Being told as soon as a new errata is released will help you plan the patching cycle, especially if the errata contains security fixes.

Staging

When applying patches and errata to your organization's systems, it is vital to know that the new updates do not cause any adverse effects to any running systems. To reduce that risk, it makes sense to stage your updates. What I mean by this is that your patching should have a flow from your lowest priority systems to your highest priority systems. You would start by patching your lowest priority systems, like a sandbox environment. Run automated testing or have a testing team sign the platform off to confirm nothing has broken during the latest patch cycle. Once you have the confidence that nothing has been affected by the new patch releases, you can proceed with your next environment (Figure 3-3).

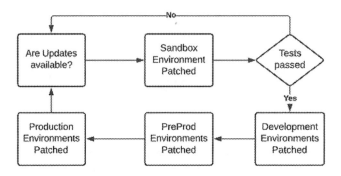

Figure 3-3. *Typical patching flow*

The example flow diagram only takes into consideration tests after the sandbox environment and does not consider packages that are different in different platforms. For this setup, it would be beneficial to have automated tests all the way through to preproduction environments. As preproduction should be a mirror of production, you are best positioned after preproduction has been patched to know if anything will break in production after patching has been completed.

Patch Management Systems

Using a patch management platform like Spacewalk or Red Hat Satellite will help with managing patch management cycles. These systems are built with functionality that allow sysadmins to ring fence patches or errata to never reach an environment.

Satellite 6, for example, has the ability to group the packages and errata that are downloaded. These groups of packages and errata are then version controlled and pushed to specific environments. These groups of updates can then be migrated between the various environments, allowing you, the sysadmin, to decide what environment gets what updates. Something very useful if you have "trigger happy" users constantly trying to run "yum update" on the systems they use. Hopefully, this is never the case, but sometimes mistakes can happen, and it is useful to be able to avoid unnecessary downtime by not having updates available in the first place.

Table 3-1 lists a few of the commonly used patch management systems used today.

Table 3-1. *Patch management systems*

System Name	What Is It Used For?
Red Hat Satellite	Used for RHEL 6 and up systems. Can be used for patching and system provisioning plus more.
SUSE Manager	Used for SUSE systems and can be used for patching and system provisioning.

Note   In the next chapter, I will discuss the Satellite server a bit more in detail. If you want to know more, I recommend reading some of the official documentation for more information.

Planning

Patch planning sounds like something you would do in your sleep, and as most organizations do their patching out of hours, this is probably what happens when the systems are being updated.

Having a solid plan for system patching is almost as important as the patching itself. This plan would allow all systems to be patched in a timely fashion and avoid the risk of systems not getting updates in time and being exposed to the vulnerabilities they were designed to avoid.

A good patching plan should include how patches are applied, where the patches are coming from (patch management system), how to check the patches were installed, and, most importantly, how to back out the patch in the event of system issues. If the plan is foolproof, the implementation can be done by less experienced sysadmins, allowing the workload to be spread.

Rollback

When the rare occurrence occurs of a system patch causing more harm than it fixes, you will need to know how to roll back the system to a working state. This can be done in a few ways.

System Restore from Backup

Before making any changes to a system, it is good practice to back up the system. This would involve backing up the filesystem files and directories most important to your system. Restoring from these backups will get you back to the state you were in before the updates, but it must be understood this process can be quite time consuming and if patching out of hours could be time you do not have.

Restore Snapshot

Virtual machines can be snapshotted, and typically it is a quick process. Restoring from a snapshot can sometimes take longer if the snapshot has been running for a longer time, but typically this process takes seconds.

Package Management Rollback

Another relatively quick rollback method is to use the package management system to roll back. With Red Hat Enterprise Linux or any distro that uses yum, you have the ability to roll back using the "`yum history undo <id>`" command. Other distros like Ubuntu and SUSE are a bit more complicated.

Reinstallation of Packages

The slightly more irritating approach would be the removal and reinstallation of the defective package. The problem with this approach is the discovery process to find the offending package would take most of your time if you are patching a large number of packages and systems. Although this would solve the problem, you will be spending time you may not have during your patch window.

Redeployment of System

The sledgehammer approach would be to blow away the system and redeploy. Something that can be done in lower priority systems like sandpit but definitely not something most organizations will do in production.

Backup and Recovery

Backing up your Linux systems is something you would ordinarily do if you build systems that cannot be redeployed easily. The idea of redeploying a system from code is far more appealing to organizations today than restoring from backup. However, there may be systems that cannot be redeployed so easily in the event of disaster. For those systems, you will need to know what directories and files are important to back up. You will need to understand how to restore from these backups and finally what the best options are for faster recovery.

Important Directories and Files

There are some standard directories that are important to back up if you need to back up at a filesystem level. These directories should include but not be limited to the following:

```
/etc
/home
/root
/usr
/opt
/svr
/var (be sure to exclude logs or anything large not required)
```

The preceding directories should be compressed with your tool of choice. That archive can then be pushed to a backup location. This can be any storage type you wish; just remember that some backup locations over a network could take longer than others. If you need the backups completed within a certain window, choose wisely.

Virtual Machine Backups

Most virtual machine providers have the ability to snapshot virtual machines. Snapshots however are not backups. Snapshots are there for you to use for quick recovery while you are working on the system. Snapshots can grow quite large as they keep track of everything the system changes; if those changes are not kept in check, they can cause you a bit of a problem when you need to reconsolidate the changes later.

There are a few methods of backing up virtual machines, but most of them basically copy the disk image of the virtual machine. Some third-party software can manage this for you so you are able to back up live virtual machines, but they come at a premium. Standard virtual machine backups would require the virtual machine to be shut down first, which is not always possible.

Virtualization platform managers should have solutions in place, but in the event of no backups being done, ensure that you at least take snapshots when doing potential destructive work.

Disaster Recovery

As an organization, it is vital that production platforms remain up as much as possible. This could involve many different solutions and should involve redundancy at all levels. When those plans fail in the completely unprepared scenario, there needs to be a plan to recover from disaster. The goal of disaster recovery is not to ensure all single points of failure are covered but more how to return back to production.

Best Strategies Based on Recovery Times

Let's explore a few disaster recovery options and discuss which ones could suit your organization.

Replicated Data Centers

As much as running out of multiple data centers is a good idea, it too can sometimes not be enough to avert disaster. Where multiple data centers can work and allow true disaster recovery would be if both data centers were mirrors of each other. Data would need to be constantly replicated, and systems would need to be identical on both sides, or at least as close as possible. This solution effectively means doubling up on all costs and would require good quality connectivity between both data centers.

Stretched Clusters

Technically, this is not a disaster recovery solution but does allow the ability for data centers to be failover between each other, allowing reduced downtime and giving the ability to switch data centers when maintenance is required.

This solution, however, does require infrastructure that can be clusters. Everything from storage through to networking equipment will need to be configured in such a way that failover is possible.

Infrastructure As Code

As most organizations have already started to embrace the world of automation, this method of disaster recovery should not seem completely strange.

If everything deployed and configured in your estate is automated, all that would need to be recovered to continue operating would be the code to execute your automation. If this is backed up and restored across data centers or cloud platforms, the automation could then be run to rebuild all systems required by your organization. This approach would require a high degree of organization and would involve a strict build process that only allows systems to be built from code.

There is the element of actual data that would need to be restored in the event of disaster, which in itself would need a complete book written on the subject to address all the complexities involved in creating the perfect solution.

Cloud

Very much like having another data center, using cloud platforms like AWS or Azure can provide an excellent platform for disaster recovery. Having an entire cloud platform automated to build a replica of our on-premise systems could provide an ideal fast failover. Ideally, this platform if not used for production could be turned off to save costs. Then in the event of disaster, the cloud environment could be powered and traffic redirected while issues on-premise are resolved. This solution would require massive investment on your part to ensure configuration is replicated from the on-premise systems, and you would still need to work out how data can be replicated to ensure no data is lost. Out of all the disaster recovery options, this one could be one of the cheaper options, as once the platform is built, it could be powered off. Factoring only data costs and the cost of reserving IP addresses, the cloud platform could potentially lie dormant until required.

Common Bad Practices

Before looking at a few good practices for estate management, let's look at some examples of some not so good practices.

Virtual Machine Templates

Previously, we spoke about using virtual machine templates to build Linux systems. This in itself is not a bad practice, but the neglect of maintaining the templates can be. Using a single template and not patching it or resolving vulnerabilities can leave your estate open to deploying systems that will fail compliance scanning.

If you use virtual machine templates as your Linux build process, ensure that you keep on top of keeping your templates in order. Build a regular schedule job into your work plan that cannot be skipped for someone to check the state of the templates and ensure they remain up to date.

Patching or Lack Thereof

Sometimes, system patching falls behind and on very rare occasions gets forgotten. Having systems up to date is extremely important if systems are accessible from the outside world. It goes without saying that if a known vulnerability is not patched on your system, you are potentially opening yourself and your organization up for disaster. Even platforms not accessible from the outside world should be patched and updated regularly. These systems seem secure, but if an intruder were even able to access your network, having all your systems as secure as possible would at least make it harder for any further damage to be done.

Firewall Disabled

Local Linux firewalls can be a pain to maintain and configure when running thousands of systems, but their importance cannot be stressed enough. Just like patching systems in a secure network reduces the risk of further damage if an intruder did even manage to breach your network, local Linux firewalls could provide another inconvenience for the would-be intruder.

Automate the firewall configuration on build and use configuration management platforms to ease the pain of managing these firewalls. They could make the difference one day.

SELinux Disabled or Permissive

More often than not, when I visit new customers, I find they have disabled SELinux or not set SELinux to enforcing mode on their systems, sometimes due to the fact that they don't know how to configure SELinux or haven't understood the benefits.

Having as many options available to ensure a system remains secure can only be an advantage to any organization. Setting SELinux to enforcing mode is often a requirement of compliance scanning. Getting used to using SELinux now will make life that much better when you are forced to enable it later.

Using Community Repositories

Using enterprise Linux distributions like Red Hat Enterprise Linux is not restricted to only using Red Hat repositories. Community repositories like EPEL can be enabled and used if you want to. Sometimes, this is for a good reason like requiring a package not available in Red Hat repositories, and sometimes it can be enabled because an organization wishes to use cutting-edge packages, which, when supported by yourself entirely and your organization, is fine. It is not okay though if you are reliant on using enterprise support. The problem would be potentially contaminating a system to the extent that it became unsupported until you remove nonsanctioned packages and updates. This could provide major headaches when raising support cases when you have problems in production.

Scripts, Scripts, and More Scripts

Using bash or shell scripts to manage your platform can seem like a great idea but can easily spin out of control. New starters and leavers all create their own scripts, and soon before you know it, no one knows what is used for what anymore. Worse than that, some of these scripts are less than desirable and in some cases are outright dangerous.

Management platforms should be used as much as possible, and all scripts should be in the form of automation executed from an automation platform.

Running As Root

Logging in to a system as root is not something anyone should be doing in a production environment. Production does not always mean customer-facing systems either. Development environments with developers actively working can also be regarded as production. Logging in directly as root removes any audit trails and gives full permissions for someone to accidentally cause an issue. Always log in with your own credentials and su to root if you need to. This practice needs to be followed by everyone and not just standard users.

Good Practices

The following are some of my personal opinions on what constitutes estate management good practices.

Building Throwaway Systems

Any system you build should be built in such a way that it could be possible to delete and redeploy. Yes, some systems will take time to redeploy, but if built in a standard repeatable way from a trusted source, you should have the confidence to throw any system away and redeploy. Changing your personal and organization's culture into a cloud-oriented working model will help and drive innovation. Firefighting and troubleshooting should be reduced, freeing you up to spend more time doing things that interest you more.

Automate As Much As Possible

This one's self-explanatory, but whenever possible try to automate what you do. The idea of manually doing anything today just seems strange as chances are you will need to repeat the job at one point or the other. Having automation in place just streamlines everything and also provides a good source of documentation for any new starters. Besides, writing automation code is far more exciting and interesting than clicking next on an install.

Search Before Creating

Before diving head on into writing a new Ansible role or any kind of script, always do your due diligence and check if someone has not already done it for you. The chances are you will find what you are looking for and save yourself time and effort. Reinventing the wheel is just a waste of time, and in most cases the content you find has taken a while to create with a fair amount of effort and thought.

Sharing Knowledge and Collaborating

Share what you learn with your work colleagues and try to involve as many people as you can in work projects. Run workshops and build interest in what you do. This will open the door for your managers to give you more time to innovate and show your value to your organization. Please do not feel that what you learn should be kept only to yourself; you never know if someone can offer an alternative view with an interesting twist to make something better. Remember, open source is more than code available. It is collaboration and being open.

Source Control

Anything you develop to manage your estate should be stored in a source control platform like Git. The code should have code review done and should absolutely never be executed in production until rigorous testing has been done. We all have the best intentions when we write code and can often be blinded by the mistakes we make. A second pair of eyes can sometimes be all the difference.

Reassessing System Requirements

When running a large virtual machine estate, the resources required may not always reflect the resources requested for the original builds. Using estate monitoring tooling will help you stay on top of systems that don't actually require the resources they were allocated. This could allow you to free up the unused resources for other systems. This of course will not matter too much if your virtualization platform was configured to reclaim unused resources automatically.

Summary

In this chapter, you were introduced to the following topics and discussion points:

- Some outdated ways of working that have been adopted over the years. Things to avoid

- The Linux build process and how it can be improved. What are some of the problems that can be encountered and what can be done to improve the process

- The processes involved in Linux system patching and the importance of staying up to date

- Backup and recovery options including ideas around disaster recovery

- Common bad practices and things that should ideally not be done when managing Linux estates

- Good practices and recommendations on things to start doing

CHAPTER 4

Estate Management Tools

Managing larger Linux estates can be challenging if not done properly. Trying to manage thousands of Linux systems following techniques and tooling from 20 years ago will leave you in a heap of trouble, none so much when compliance scanning shows holes in your environment. Not only will you find mass amounts of security vulnerabilities that could give any security person heart palpitations, it will also leave you with a depressing amount of remediation work.

To avoid these issues, the use of management software is highly recommended. Even with a modest amount of Linux systems to manage, management platforms will only make life easier. The day-to-day tasks can be automated, the build process streamlined, and the dreaded security remediation offloaded to the management platform to handle for you.

Some tooling does come with a cost, and for that reason, it is important to also know what community options are available. Very much like we discussed in the earlier chapters, we will do a similar comparison. The idea behind this chapter is to get you familiar with management platforms, what they are used for, and how they can make your life easier as a Linux sysadmin.

© Kenneth Hitchcock 2022
K. Hitchcock, *Linux System Administration for the 2020s*,
https://doi.org/10.1007/978-1-4842-7984-7_4

Management Systems

There are two kinds of management systems we will look at in this chapter: Linux platform management systems and automation platforms. For each type of management system, I will explain what the system does and the basic concepts of the tool. To be very clear from the start, this book is not an official guide on how to use these platforms. All I am trying to do is get you familiar with what the tools do and how they could benefit you.

Linux Platform Tools

The first and most important management tool you should be using if you are not already using one is the Linux platform management tool. This tool is the center of your estate and controls a big part of what Linux sysadmins should be doing. This tool should have some if not all of the following functionality:

- Package syncing from external repositories

- Ability to segregate packages by environment

- Linux build and kickstart capabilities

- Compliance scanning and reporting

- Configuration drift control

- Platform monitoring and logging

- Integration into virtualization or cloud platforms

- Ability to work in a disconnected environment

- Must be scalable and reliable

Obviously, you don't always need all the preceding functionality, but it does help to have the features available in case you start evolving your ways of working. An example of this could be your organization's decision to start using more cloud facilities. Having a tool with cloud provisioning abilities will save you having to use another platform or writing your own.

Linux Platform Tools Available

Table 4-1 provides a list of some of the more common Linux platform tools you can use to manage small to large Linux estates.

Table 4-1. *Linux platform management options*

Product	Description
Red Hat Satellite	The premier enterprise Linux estate management tool from Red Hat. Used to manage estates of RHEL 6 and upward. The product has been around for almost two decades at the time of writing
Foreman	A community product used for managing the Linux system build process. Foreman is the upstream for Red Hat Satellite 6
Katello	A community product that provides content management for Foreman. Katello is another product used by Red Hat Satellite 6 as its upstream equivalent
Pulp	A community product that manages package repositories for Linux systems. Pulp like Foreman and Katello is another upstream product for Red Hat Satellite 6
SUSE Manager	The enterprise product from SUSE to manage SUSE platforms. SUSE Manager is based on the community product Uyuni, which in itself is a fork of the Spacewalk project

(*continued*)

Table 4-1. (*continued*)

Product	Description
Spacewalk	Spacewalk has in the past been used as the upstream for Red Hat Satellite 5. Today, it remains a community Linux platform management tool that has been abandoned by its developers
Uyuni	A community platform management system that provides system provisioning and patch management capabilities. Configuration management is managed by SaltStack and features the ability to run compliance scanning. Uyuni is a fork of the Spacewalk product with integrated SaltStack. Uyuni is also the upstream for SUSE Manager
EuroLinux	Another community Linux estate management tool which appears to be also forked from Spacewalk with SaltStack integration

Note   The Spacewalk forked platforms are mostly the same other than the inclusion of SaltStack. If you decide to use one of them, the decision will need to be based on product fix frequency to ensure you have bug fixes and vulnerability patching available.

Selecting Your Linux Platform Tool

With most things in the open source world, there are enterprise products and community products. Depending on your organization's requirements and budget restrictions, you may be limited in your choices. To understand how to make the correct decision on which tool you should be using, let's look at what you need to ask yourself:

- Support: Do I need support from an enterprise vendor if I encounter issues, or am I happy to work with communities and their forums to get my answer?

- Linux distros: What Linux distributions am I managing? Do they have enterprise subscriptions that need to be managed?

- Features: What features can I not do without? Am I happy to use multiple platforms to provide all the features I want, or do I require a tool that has everything in one place?

The Decision

The product you use will be heavily weighted by your organization's needs. Often, regulatory compliance will dictate if you use enterprise vs. community products. Feature the product should have, tend to be dictated by decision makers above you who do not understand what you as a Linux sysadmin does or what the products do, leaving you potentially with a product that will be more of a hindrance than a help.

My advice with the above is to build a case for the product you feel is correct not only for you but your organization. For that, you will need to be decisive in your decision and show a clear good reason or reasons for why the product you prefer to use is the best for the job. If the product is an enterprise product, you will also need to justify costs and prove it is better than its competitors. Depending on your company's way of working, a presentation with advantages and disadvantages should be a useful exercise, possibly with a comparison of features between different products.

To support your decision and to build your case, you must be confident the product is the right product for you. To do this, you must be familiar with it and understand its limitations. This can be achieved by doing the following:

- Have the vendor demo the product: If the product is a paid-for product, ask the vendor to come visit you. Request a demo of the product to be shown to you and your company's decision makers. This will increase your chances of getting the product you want if it has more visibility within your organization. Decision makes will then have all the information available to them to make an informed decision.

- Proof of concept: Another useful way to understand how a platform tool works is by building a proof of concept system to test. If you are wanting to test an enterprise product, speak to the vendor and request a demo subscription or license. Community products normally do not require subscriptions, but some might require or request a donation.

Tip   It is advisable to test a slightly older version of a community product for your PoC testing. This should reduce some pain that can come from bleeding edge technologies. Stick to stable branches when you are still learning.

Satellite Server

The first and probably the one most people will know is the Red Hat flagship management system: Red Hat Satellite server. Originally released in 2002, Satellite was based on the upstream Spacewalk community project until Satellite 6.x was released in 2014. Since then, Satellite 6 has been based on a number of upstream products all combined together to provide the latest Red Hat platform management system.

Satellite 5

Red Hat Satellite 5.x worked quite well as an overall Linux estate management system. Satellite provided patch management, system deployment, compliance scanning, configuration management, and general estate management functionality.

Some interesting points I always ended up spending more time on were around system deployment and configuration management. Both were problematic in one way or another to use.

Configuration Management

Over the course of its life, Satellite 5.x improved from version to version but had one major issue: its configuration management system. This attempt at configuration management was just awful. The configuration management used a concept of storing configuration files that would be pushed to client systems. Unfortunately, this had the habit of sprawling into chaos as more and more config files were stored. The config could be versioned, but it was extremely painful to manage and often ended up in a real mess.

System Deployment

The system deployment used in early Satellite used Cobbler along with PXE boot mechanisms. Getting the deployment system to work sometimes proved to be quite challenging at times. I spent many hours tweaking config to get systems to deploy only to later find out I didn't set correct permissions or I was missing a package. Later versions improved and became easier to install. Possibly a combination of me gaining experience and the documentation improving.

Satellite 6

The current major release of the Satellite server is version 6.x. Satellite 6.x is based on a combination of products including the following:

- Foreman
- Katello
- Pulp
- Hammer
- Candlepin

Content Management

The best feature for me that was introduced with Satellite 6 was the complete overhaul of the content management system. Previously in Satellite 5 and in Spacewalk systems, the content was segregated into "channels." These "channels" required cloning from one to the other to create a staging flow for you to apply content from dev to test to production. If this doesn't make sense, don't worry; it confused enough people when I tried to show them in the past. I will break it down a bit more in the "Spacewalk" section a bit later to explain a bit more.

Content Views

Fortunately, Satellite 6.x has provided a better solution with the help of Katello. The new system no longer uses "channels" but instead uses a new concept called "content views." A "content view" is a collection of content that Satellite can provide to a system. This content can contain puppet modules, Ansible roles, or standard yum repositories. Where a "content view" really shines is in its ability to be versioned. This means, as new packages are downloaded on Satellite or new puppet modules are added, the "content views" previously versioned are unaffected. Meaning any systems allocated to these "content views" will not see the new content. Perfect if you wish to stage your content through your life cycles.

Tip As content views grow, they can take longer to publish. Keeping the content view small can help with this, or you can enable download on demand.

Life Cycles

Content views are useful to group content, but they do need to be used by systems. To do that, registered systems are added to different life cycles. These life cycles can be called whatever you like, but generally they are given boring names as follows:

Library (Default) ➤ Development ➤ Test UAT ➤ Pre Production ➤ Production

Content views are then associated with life cycles which in turn are associated systems.

Content Management Flow

A basic example of content being updated and being applied to a life cycle environment is shown in Figure 4-1.

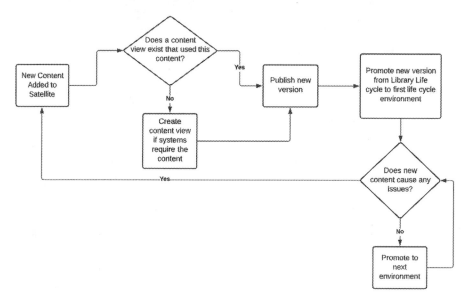

Figure 4-1. *Typical life cycle environment*

The basic flow in Figure 4-1 shows how content views are updated, published, and pushed into different life cycle environments, thus allowing the migration of content like package updates or errata to be moved from test through to production environments.

Tip   Content views can be nested. They are called composite content views.

System Provisioning

With the introduction of using Foreman instead of Cobbler, the Linux deployment process has been simplified in one extent and complicated in another. The complexity has mostly been brought in around ensuring that organizations and locations have been configured for all components of the provisioning process. Things like "operating systems" and "network subnets" all need to be added to the correct "organization" and "location." Once you have gotten your head around the grouping issues, the rest of the configuration becomes a bit more straightforward than the previous Cobbler configuration.

One major thing to note about the system provisioning process is that when you deploy your Satellite, you do need to ensure that you add the features for system deployment. The official Red Hat documentation explains the process quite clearly and provides all the parameters you will need. If you prefer to not use the documentation, you can also look at the "`satellite-installer --help`" command for more parameters. They are self-explanatory and should make sense when you see them. My recommendation is to stick to the official documentation when you install your Satellite for the first time. Once you have one done, the help command is useful to remind you of what you need.

System Patching

Patching systems registered to Satellite are no different to previous Satellite versions. The systems still need to run "yum update" to get the latest content. Remote execution can also be used like it used to be used in Satellite 5.x for mass execution across the entire estate. Personally, I would recommend using your automation platform to do this, but this would be up to you on how you wish to manage your estate.

The biggest change from previous Satellite versions remains around the "content view" versions. When new content is available and you wish to deploy across your estate, remember to follow the content management flow diagram further up in the chapter. Once your "content view" has been promoted to your system's life cycle environments, you will be able to execute your system updates.

Configuration Management

Configuration management has drastically been improved with Satellite 6 from Satellite 5. Early versions of Satellite 6.x only used "Puppet" for configuration management and SOE (Standard Operating Environment). One downside of Puppet is that Puppet requires puppet agents running on client systems. These agents often need to be configured to check in to the Satellite Puppet master to ensure they are kept in line with expected configuration.

The Puppet content would be stored within the "content view" associated with the client system registered to the Satellite server. The Puppet client would then check in with the Satellite Puppet master and would then run through the content available to check if anything new needs to be applied or corrected. If the Puppet agent was stopped on the client system, the configuration would not be applied.

Later versions of Satellite 6 introduced Ansible as another option for configuration management, which, very similar to Puppet configuration, required a "content view" to contain all the Ansible roles and configuration you wished your system to be configured with.

The Puppet or Ansible configuration would also be version controlled with "content views" and would also require publishing and promoting for updated content to be made available to the systems registered to Satellite.

Reasons to Use Satellite

- Ability to provision RHEL systems with an easier-to-use provisioning platform

- Ability to stage patching and updates across environments

- Enterprise product with continued support and feature enhancements

- Integrated compliance scanning and remediation

- Configuration management with Puppet or Ansible

Reasons to Not Use Satellite

- Costs involved could be out of range for a small organization.

- Not recommended for tiny estates of less than 30 systems or so.

- Not ideal for non-Red Hat systems.

SUSE Manager

SUSE Manager 4.x is the latest SUSE Linux platform management tool. SUSE Manager 4.x is based on the community product Uyuni (ya - uni).

Uyuni

Uyuni was originally forked from the Spacewalk project but started to divert so much from the original Spacewalk project that it has started to become a tool of its own, which is refreshing to know as Spacewalk has been around for a long time and had its fair share of issues.

Where Spacewalk failed with its poor configuration management, Uyuni excelled by scrapping the old configuration management tool and replacing it with SaltStack. This decision was a stroke of genius and possibly a good decision why Uyuni is the SUSE Manager upstream project.

Support

Uyuni and SUSE Manager have their own challenges I'm sure, and those with more experience with this tool may know all about them. The SUSE Manager configuration is not drastically too dissimilar to Red Hat Satellite and is self-explanatory. Both products have excellent documentation and provide enterprise support.

SUSE Manager Configuration

One of the first things that needs to be done with SUSE Manager is to register your account so packages can be synced for your SUSE environments, very much like Red Hat Satellite. The downloaded content is then sorted into "channels," which is the same concept used from Spacewalk. A new concept of life cycles has been introduced which improves how the added content can be managed to provide updates across environments. This new approach streamlines the process instead of having to do the "channel" sync that Spacewalk used to require.

If you are a SUSE organization, SUSE Manager 4 is the tool you should consider using for your environment. Read the official documentation, build a proof of concept system, and compare its functionality with what else is available.

Reasons to Use SUSE Manager

- You can provision SUSE systems with a central provisioning platform.

- Ability to stage patching and updates across environments.

- Enterprise product with continued support and feature enhancements.

- Configuration management with SaltStack.

Reasons to Not Use SUSE Manager

- Where costs exceed the usefulness

- Using non-SUSE distros that need to be managed

- Managing a small estate of less than 30 or so systems

Foreman

Foreman is one of the main upstream projects for Red Hat Satellite 6.x. The main function of Foreman is to assist with the provisioning of Linux systems; however, Foreman does have the ability to be extended in its functionality by adding plugins.

Provision Hypervisors

One nice feature of Foreman is that it has the ability to provision not only Linux platforms but also virtualization hypervisors. A very handy ability if you are looking at automating your estate to the "nth" degree.

Plugins

Foreman, however, by itself does not assist in content management or configuration management like Satellite 6.x. For that, you will need to combine Foreman with extra plugins. The plugins range from Katello for content management all the way through to configuration management and automation with Chef. As Foreman is a community project, new plugins are being made available all the time, and the functionality is constantly growing.

Open Source Does Need Money Too

Foreman is a community product that does not require subscriptions or licensing. The project does accept donations if you like what they are doing. If you are up for it, you can contribute to the project and provide some valuable resource in any way you can.

Spacewalk

As the management tool that started it all for Linux platform management, Spacewalk deserved to be mentioned, be it only briefly.

Abandoned

Spacewalk unfortunately has been abandoned by its developers and has been left to others to fork and evolve the project. Uyuni is one such project that has taken what Spacewalk started and is currently building quite a nice-looking tool. Canonical, the Ubuntu distro company, is another that is using a Spacewalk variation for its platform management.

Why It Was Good

What made Spacewalk such a great product at the time was its ability to manage Linux systems at large. Systems could be grouped, and remote execution could be sent to all the systems at once, a very useful ability when you had hundreds of systems to patch or to install packages. This was before the days of Ansible and even Puppet slightly. As mentioned a few times, the Spacewalk configuration management was awful to use, but it did provide functionality to keep configuration in line if you did not run a

Puppet environment. As Puppet was on the slightly difficult side to master and understand, configuration management in Spacewalk was a nice tool to have even if it was not the best.

Network Provisioning

Spacewalk also introduced more people to Cobbler and kickstart deployment, taking Linux system building to a new era of deployment. Having the ability to boot a system off the network and selecting a kickstart file to use really took some of the pain away from running around with physical media. The fact that the kickstart files would automate the install made life even easier, and those who were up for the challenge could create their own snippets of code to configure the newly built system that bit further.

Environment Staging

Environment management with channels meant that package cloning could ensure that environments did not get updates unless the Linux sysadmins deemed it so. This was the same with errata and bug fixes.

Thank You for Your Service

Spacewalk served its purpose well for a long time, but with the introduction of Foreman and other such products, it has come time for Spacewalk to retire as it was. New versions like Uyuni have taken what Spacewalk was and evolved it into something new and exciting again.

Provisioning Tools

Another type of management system that can be used to manage your estate is a dedicated provisioning tool. Technically, Foreman is a provisioning tool and so is Satellite, but a dedicated provisioning tool would act as a single interface into all aspects of your portfolio. If you deployed on-premise in the cloud, having a provisioning tool would mean that all operations could be executed from one location.

Cloudforms

Red Hat Cloudforms is an enterprise provisioning tool based on the ManageIQ upstream project. Red Hat acquired ManageIQ in December of 2012 and continued to drive the adoption of Cloudforms through the next decade.

Single Pane of Glass

Cloudforms has always been described as the single pane of glass into your estate. Cloudforms has the ability to integrate into VMware, RHV, and various cloud providers like AWS and Azure for provisioning but also could integrate with Red Hat Satellite and Ansible Tower, giving you even more control of your estate.

State Machines

With the integration options available, virtual machines and cloud instances can be created with what is known as a "state machine." A "state machine" is written with Ruby on rails code to provide the automation steps required to build and configure your virtual machine or cloud instance. In the newer releases of Cloudforms, the ability to use Ansible instead of Ruby on rails has become available.

A rather large downside of state machine development was the complex setup required to get it to work. This was not something that came out of the box and often required someone with experience to assist in getting it to work. Even then, the process was still complicated.

User Request Portal

Cloudforms or ManageIQ has the ability to be used as a provisioning request portal, which if configured can be restricted for nontechnical users to use and request platforms without knowing anything about the underlying configuration required. Custom forms and screens can be configured to allow nontechnical users to fill in and request systems. Behind these simple screens are the state machines and automation configured to execute the tasks.

Chargeback

Another really nice facility is the ability to control chargeback for any systems that are being built in the estate. Cost centers or similar can be configured to manage estate costs and can be billed to different teams or departments.

Request Approvals

When users request a new system or platform, approvals can be configured that need to be passed before any automation can be executed. Multiple layers of approvals can also be configured, allowing change control teams to approve builds. Something very useful if you want to stay in control of what is built.

Advantages

- Very simple to install as Cloudforms is deployed from a template appliance.

- Cloudforms is a feature-rich tool with many possibilities.

- Ability to interface with many systems and provide a single management tool to manage them all.

- Complete data centers can be provisioned once the appliance has been deployed.

- Custom user portals can be used for users to request systems.

- Integration with platforms like ServiceNow.

Disadvantages

- Cloudforms has a steep technical learning curve.

- The configuration is not the easiest to understand, and it takes time getting used to it, but once users are familiar with it, the possibilities are endless.

- Feature development has also been slowing down in recent years, possibly indicating that the end for the product is near.

Terraform

Terraform is another interesting product to use if you wish to provision to different platforms. Provided by HashiCorp, Terraform is an open source infrastructure as code solution that has the ability to provision across multiple environments such as AWS or Azure.

Products Available

HashiCorp provides a few options for using Terraform outside of their enterprise support.

Community CLI

There is the standard community CLI option that is available to everyone who wishes to learn and use it. Most if not all Terraform functionality is available for you to start using the platform from day one.

Terraform Cloud Platform

Another way of using Terraform for free is through the "free" tier of the Terraform cloud solution. This is a HashiCorp managed service that offers some basic functionality in the free tier but also offers extended features for some of the paid-for services.

API and Extracting Useful Information

With all the management tools available today, it can become quite cumbersome to use different tools for different jobs. To get around this, I have seen some organizations build their own "abstraction" layer. This layer typically is a custom application written using Python or similar development language that communicates with other management platforms through their API.

Don't Reinvent the Wheel

There are tools already available that can connect to other systems through their API. Cloudforms and ManageIQ are tools that can be used off the shelf to do quite a bit of the API integration to other platforms. The only downside to these tools is that they are structured more around deployment of systems. Automation and patching type tasks might need a bit tweaking to get going.

Why to Not Write Your Own Tool

Writing your own custom tool that leverages different tools through their API does have some major advantages, but it comes with the heavy price of internal development. This cost of time and effort often ends any potential chance of anything being created. Even if an organization does authorize the time and effort, another major blocker could be the lack of skills in house to develop this product. This would mean further training or time required to skill up.

Best Tools to Use

The best tools to use for API access would be something that gives you the ability to connect to the platform and have the functionality displayed in a way that makes sense to you out of the box. Does this tool exist? Unfortunately not. This is why people have traditionally written their own API calling tools and mapped the API requests to application functionality. If you are looking for a tool to reduce your development effort, you could use some of the following.

Pipeline Tooling

Jenkins or Tekton could be a useful way of connecting to the management systems API to automate deployments or system patching. The API calls can be triggered, and the events could be caught; from that, different logic could be used to determine next actions. This could be an interesting way to introduce self-healing capabilities in your estate.

Automation Platforms

Using Ansible or similar is a cleaner and better approach to contacting the management systems API. Ansible, for example, has plenty modules available that already speak to different management tools through their API. An example of this is the new Satellite modules that are now available for users to automate Satellite configuration. Something useful for managing your patching cycles when you can automate the promotion and publishing of content views.

Shell Scripts

Not the best solution but it is something you could use if all you wanted to do was automate some basic tasks. Personally, I would not take this approach; I would rather write some Ansible to do the work for me.

Summary

In this chapter, you were introduced to the following:

- Linux estate management platforms to streamline the Linux build process, patching, and configuration management

- The different estate management tools available today and why to use or not to use them

- Cloud provisioning tools like Cloudforms, ManageIQ, and Terraform

- Using the management tooling API to streamline their usage and build their functionality into your day-to-day automation

CHAPTER 5

Automation

This is the first chapter in which we will target a specific discipline, automation.

In this chapter, we will delve into the dark arts of manipulating systems by the hundreds if not thousands. We will discuss what the best tools are and why you should use them or avoid them. We will look at how these tools differ from each other so you can make an informed decision of which tool works best for you. We will then look at what the market trends are for these products and why some people prefer one tool over the other.

This chapter discusses automation in general and does not focus on one particular product. The idea is to understand the concepts of automation and how they should be applied in the best possible way. We will discuss topics such as "when you should automate vs. when you should not." We will explore using techniques to automate automation and when that should be done.

Finally, we will end the chapter discussing best practices and using shell scripting, in which we will discuss different shell scripting languages that can be used.

Automation in Theory

Automation should not be anything new to most people reading this. There has always been some form of automation in what we have done in the past, be it custom shell scripts or some management tool scheduled to kick off a job.

© Kenneth Hitchcock 2022
K. Hitchcock, *Linux System Administration for the 2020s*,
https://doi.org/10.1007/978-1-4842-7984-7_5

Automation has evolved quite a bit over the last decade, with new tooling and automation platforms being developed. The days of using custom scripts that are executed from cron jobs are coming to an end if not already. Complex automation solutions are now managing everything from system builds to self-healing systems.

Automation does not only have to be technical either. Most organizations are now looking at solutions to automate business processes along with their technical estate management. Building in automation to create change requests or raise support tickets is becoming more a requirement than a luxury. The time and effort saved is what brings more organizations to the realization that having no full-stack automation in the pipeline spells disaster for keeping up with competitors.

Idempotent Code

The number one thing that all automation should be adhering to is ensuring that the code written is idempotent. This effectively means that the code will only make a change if the state does not match the required state from the automation platform.

An example of this could be updating a system package. If the system has a package installed that is already at the latest version, you would not want the automation task to do anything except confirm the package is at the version requested. By not doing anything but confirming the state of the package, the system remains untouched. If the package required a service restart, the reinstallation or updating of the package could have resulted in a tiny outage. This is possibly a poor example as handles can also be used to ensure there are no outages.

Always remember when writing automation code:

"Is my code idempotent?"

Knowing When and When Not to Automate

Half the battle when writing automation code is knowing what to automate and what should not be automated. My general rule of thumb has always been to automate anything I'm going to repeat at some point, which with my line of work is always on the cards.

It seems obvious to write automation only for repeatable tasks, but what about writing automation to build something that is only needed once? This can be a bad thing if not thought out to why you are doing it, but it can also make perfect sense.

"After spending all that time getting your automation to work, you could have just installed the system yourself manually and saved a heap of time."

This could be the typical thing your manager could say to you when they find out how much effort went into writing the code you wrote for something that will only be built once.

The argument you should follow up with to why automating something that will only be used once is the fact that you are building the estate from code and you are preparing for possible rebuilds in the event of disaster.

According to Gartner, organizations that don't automate are likely to see a 25% drop in their customer retention. Automation is rapidly growing everywhere, and if you or your organization falls behind, you are at risk of being outrun by your competitors.

To fully understand when or when not to automate, let's look at some reasons for and against automation.

Reasons to Automate

To automate should be the default today; however, if you need reasons, here are a few worth mentioning:

- Repeatable and predictable builds

- Infrastructure as code

- Code as documentation

- Time and cost savings

- Organizational culture change

- Reduced risk

- To encourage innovation

Reasons Not to Automate

It is hard to think of reasons not to automate anything today, but sometimes there are reasons, even if they are not very good ones:

- A single task that won't ever be repeated. Even then, there are reasons to automate this too.

- Organization has not matured yet to accept automation.

- No skills available or time for training.

These preceding points are not really good reasons, but more excuses in my personal opinion. The world of estate management and estate building is rapidly changing today, and not automating should not be an option. As Linux sysadmins, our job has changed whether we like it or not. We no longer are Linux sysadmins, we are now automation engineers.

State Management

Another very important thing to understand about different automation platforms is their ability to manage system state. Some platforms only check state when code is being executed for a specific task, whereas other platforms constantly check the systems they manage for its current state to see if anything has been changed. When state change is detected, the configuration is updated to match the desired state from the automation platform.

Tip   Using a platform that constantly checks system state based on desired state will ensure you run an environment that will remain standard. This is very useful when you have different people who could potentially make system changes that could cause system outages. This approach will also reduce the chance of configuration drift.

Automation Tooling

We can all agree automation is not going away anytime soon, and to not be left behind, it is important to understand what tooling you should be using. Adopting automation practices will require a set of tools and development languages that you will need to learn; which ones to use will require you to make an informed decision.

Over the next few pages, we will discuss the different options available for you today and discuss what makes them good or bad to use.

Automation Scripting Languages

Before we start looking into the different tooling, it is worth understanding the different types of automation scripting languages that can be used to write automation code: YAML, Ruby, Python, and shell scripting.

YAML

"YAML Ain't Markup Language" is the main language used by automation platforms such as Ansible and SaltStack. YAML is one of the easier scripting languages to learn as most of the syntax is quite simple to understand and remember.

These Are Not the Spaces You Are Looking For

YAML is notorious for complaining about formatting, which is one area that can annoy people when they first learn to code with YAML. The indentation needs to be 100% correct, else your code will not run.

YAML does not like the use of the tab character and only accepts standard space characters for indentation. The tab character in most editors is replaced with the corresponding number of spaces to make this process seem like the tab values have been used.

YAML in Action

The following two examples use the popular automation platforms Ansible and SaltStack. Both examples provide the same result, which is to install the "httpd" package.

Ansible

```
---
- name: "Build Linux Web server"
  hosts: webservers
  become: true

  tasks:
  - name: "Install latest apache httpd package"
    ansible.builtin.yum:
      name: httpd
      state: latest
```

SaltStack

```
websetup:
    pkg:
        - installed
        - pkgs:
            - apache2
```

These examples use similar formatting, and both are indented in a very similar way. From these examples, the logic is easily understood and fairly easily manipulated to install other packages. These examples use a basic package module provided, but many other modules are available to do so much more. A quick google search often lands you right on the latest documentation you can follow.

Ruby

Ruby is a high-level all-purpose programming language that was designed to be a true object-oriented language. Ruby is similar in ways to Perl and Python except how it handles its instance variables. Ruby keeps these variables private to the class and only exposes them through accessor methods like "attr_writer" or "attr_reader."

The following is a basic example of Ruby code. It is not often you would write Ruby code for automation tasks unless you needed to write a new function or something along those lines:

```
#!/usr/bin/ruby
def build(opt1 = "Linux", opt2 = "Windows")
    puts "The system that will be built is #{opt1}"
    puts "The system that will be built is  #{opt2}"
end
build
```

The following is an example of a puppet module code. Puppet includes two Ruby APIs for writing custom functions. There is more to a puppet module than the following, but just to give you a basic feel for what the code looks like, I thought it would be worth seeing an example:

```
class helloworld (
  $file_path = undef
){
  notify { "Hello world!": message => "I am in the
  ${environment} environment"}
  unless $file_path == undef {
    file{ $file_path :
      ensure     => file,
      content  => "I am in the ${environment} environment",
    }
  }
}
```

Python

Python is used in a few ways to automate tasks. You can use Python to write your own scripts in the same vein that you could write Ruby or any other scripting language. Python, however, tends to be used mostly for the modules or functions used by the likes of Ansible and SaltStack. Below is a snippet of some basic Python code.

```
# Python Module example
def add(x, y):
    """This application returns the result of x + y"""

    result = x + y
    return result

print("The value of my python function is", add(3,4))
```

Shell Scripting

Shell scripting can be used for automation but is not recommended, mostly due to the fact that other automation languages and tooling have such a rich array of modules that connect to most platforms through their API.

Shell scripting by default does not really work well as an idempotent scripting language. To implement idempotence would mean a fair bit of extra coding.

Note   Most of the automation code that generally gets written these days are YAML for platforms like Ansible and SaltStack. The other variations are Ruby type code for Puppet and Chef. It is not common to get down and dirty writing Ruby or Python modules.

Automation Platforms

With a basic idea of what the automation scripting languages look like, it now makes sense to talk about some of the automation tooling you can use that leverages the previously discussed scripting languages.

Automation in Estate Management Tools

In Chapter 4, we spoke about Linux platform management tools, and I mentioned that some have built-in automation tooling. In most cases and traditionally in the past, the automation facilities failed to provide enough functionality for them to be regarded as an outright automation platform. There are exceptions to this now today with updated management tooling like Uyuni which has included the use of SaltStack. How much of the SaltStack features are available remains to be tested.

However, to work around the lack of automation features that may be missing from estate management tools like Red Hat Satellite, it is recommended to look at using an automation platform that is dedicated to manage all your estate's automation needs. These platforms should include all the features for you to fully automate your estate.

Reasons to Use

- Already in place

- No budget for other tooling

- Skills in place already

- Save time

- Has a good integrated automation tool with enough features to get started

Reasons Not to Use

- Limited functionality

- Added complexity

- Require separation with RBAC

Ansible Automation Platform

Ansible is no doubt making a strong case to be the market-leading automation tool, well at least at the time of writing this book. Ansible's growth has been impressive over the last few years and has been gaining in popularity with more users and organizations each day. The growth of the community and the adoption of vendors across the board to create modules for Ansible continue to justify why many people are choosing Ansible as the automation tool of choice.

Without trying to predict the future, I firmly believe Ansible is going to be around for a while. The reason I say this is down to a few things:

1. Red Hat, which acquired Ansible in October of 2015, is fully behind Ansible and its development. There are constant improvements happening all the time, and clearly they have big plans for its future.

2. The Ansible learning curve is far more forgiving than other products in the same area. People just prefer to use something that doesn't require a master's degree to understand it.

3. Community adoption is growing almost by the day with more and more vendors providing new modules all the time.

Agentless

Ansible does not require any agents to manage its client systems. Connections are made to client systems via ssh on Linux or Unix-based systems and WinRM if connecting to a Windows system. Authentication can be done by entering the system's password when executing the Ansible or through the use of ssh keys. Most Linux sysadmins tend to use the ssh option, mostly as the connections to the Linux or Unix systems will be seamless and not prompt for a password. This could be a major irritation if you are running a playbook against a hundred systems.

If ssh keys are not a possibility, there are other options that can be used, but this would require all the systems to authenticate to a central location. Else you will be stuck with entering different passwords for different systems.

Potential Security Hole

Ansible environments can potentially have a big security hole for an estate if ssh keys are not managed correctly. If a Linux sysadmin, for example, has ssh keys on their system which can access any system in the estate, there is potentially a big problem if someone gets unauthorized access to their system. For this reason, great care needs to be taken to ensure security of this system. Using system vaults could mitigate this risk as an example.

Using Ansible

Ansible is available in both enterprise and community versions. Both enterprise and community products have two "types" of Ansible that can be installed. There is the graphical interface that can be used and a command-line version.

Command Line

In Chapter 2, we briefly discussed how the Ansible command-line tool can be installed and used. We covered how there are added benefits of installing with a package management system like Yum vs. installing via pip. We also discussed how to run some basic commands.

The Ansible command line is often referred to as Ansible Core, but the naming might be changing if not changed already. Red Hat is working hard at making Ansible better all the time and is constantly working on how Ansible can be used or integrated with other products; for this reason, the name may change to fit the usage.

One thing to remember: If you choose to use the command-line version of Ansible only, it does not matter too much if you use the community or enterprise version from a functionality point of view. Both products have the same functionality last time I checked. The biggest issue would come around support if you needed help.

Recommendation   Using the graphical tool for Ansible is the recommended approach, mainly as you have functionally not easily replicated with the command-line tool.

Graphical User Interface

What seems to be attracting new users to Ansible is the graphical user interface that can be used with Ansible Automation Platform. As with anything that gains popularity, developers look at use cases and adapt based on demand. With that, it is becoming more likely that new versions of Ansible will be driven more from the graphical tools than the command line. For this reason, the current Ansible Tower tool is the recommended approach when learning Ansible for the first time.

Reasons to Use Ansible

- Simple to learn and get started

- Growing community with massive code resources available

- Excellent documentation and examples

- Ability to manage anything you can open a remote connection to

- Flexible

- Scalable

- Enterprise support

- New features being developed that may not make it to AWX

Reasons Not to Use Ansible

- If you don't need enterprise-level products, this may not be for you.

- Ansible Tower licensing can be on the expensive side if you have thousands of systems to monitor with a small budget.

- Might not be required if you have a small number of systems to manage.

- SSH key security–related issues.

- Lack of understanding system state before tasks are executed.

AWX

When Red Hat acquired Ansible, Ansible Tower had not been open sourced. To correct this, Red Hat developers and engineers worked on open sourcing Ansible Tower as fast as possible. The resulting product is the AWX project.

AWX is almost the same as its enterprise equivalent (Ansible Tower), except for a few enterprise features. An example is role-based authentication has been excluded from the community version. If a user required these features, they would need to purchase an Ansible Tower license.

Reasons to Use AWX

- Simple to learn and get started

- Growing community with massive code resources available

- Excellent documentation and examples

- Ability to manage anything you can open a remote connection to

- Community product with no costs

- Flexible

Reasons Not to Use AWX

- If you require enterprise features, you will need to consider either Ansible Automation Platform or another product.

- Less testing and work done on AWX than there is on Ansible Tower.

- Not recommended for production environments.

- Not all security components of AWX have been through security checks like what is done with Ansible Tower.

- Direct in-place upgrades between versions are not supported.

- SSH key security–related issues.

- Lack of understanding system state before tasks are executed.

SaltStack

Another python-based configuration management tool that can be used is SaltStack. SaltStack comes in both community versions and enterprise supported versions.

Server to Client Communication

Unlike Ansible, SaltStack can be configured to run in a few ways when connecting to the system it manages:

- Direct SSH

- Agent and server

- Agent only with no management server

Remote Execution

In a similar way to how Ansible connects to systems and runs ad hoc commands, SaltStack has the ability to execute remote execution commands. This functionality is very similar in what the Satellite server currently does and what the Spacewalk server used to do.

Configuration Management

SaltStack is a bit more traditional in how configuration management has been done in the past. Configuration is managed on the SaltStack master and pushed to systems that have changed or require updated configuration. The SaltStack master system controls the state of its clients (minions) that it manages through both understanding the state the system needs to be and the events that have been triggered on the minion system that the master is watching. If anything changes that should not, the SaltStack master reverts the unauthorized changes.

Uses a Message Bus

Salt uses a different approach than some other products in that it uses a message bus ZeroMQ. When a client system or minion triggers an event, a message is created on the message bus for the master server to act on when it is ready. This method of using a message bus allows a vast number of systems to be managed by one master.

Reasons to Use SaltStack

- Less of a steep learning curve.

- Modular approach.

- Massively flexible.

- Scalable.

- Performs well at scale. Thousands of minions can be managed at the same time with quite efficient performance.

- Event-driven configuration management.

- Improved security over other products.

- Feature rich.

Reasons to Not Use SaltStack

- Due to a slower release cycle, it could potentially not be for faster moving environments.

- There have been issues in the past with modules not being able to manage their own dependencies. Requiring users to run separate virtual environments.

- Not the best support for non-Linux systems.

- Installation and configuration can be more challenging.

- Documentation can be difficult to understand and use.

Puppet

Puppet is a Ruby-based configuration management system that was used quite a bit more before the introduction of Ansible.

Red Hat and Puppet

Satellite 6.x first used Puppet for its configuration management but later introduced the choice to use Ansible. Puppet has not been removed and is still available for users who invested large amounts of time developing puppet modules, but it should not be taken for granted that Puppet's availability in Satellite will remain there forever.

Server Agent Based

Puppet requires a Puppet master to manage the state of all the systems it manages. All clients are also required to have an agent running to check in with the Puppet master.

Potential Lower Adoption

Products like Ansible and SaltStack have introduced less of a steep learning curve for users and are posing a strong threat to products like Puppet and Chef. It does not help that Red Hat has also started to introduce Ansible in as many of their products as possible to further drive the popularity of Ansible. SaltStack has also been included in newer versions of Spacewalk clones used by SUSE and Ubuntu. The popularity of these distros and their respective management software does not bode well for Puppet.

Enterprise and Community

Puppet has both community and enterprise versions available to accommodate users across the board. Enterprise support is available for corporate organizations that require support agreements for compliance or regulatory reasons, and there are community versions available for the users that do not require support.

Reasons to Use Puppet

- State-based configuration management. Clients are constantly checking in to Puppet masters for configuration changes.

- Excellent community support. Example code readily available.

- Installation is painless and simple.

- Runs on almost every operating system available.

- Idempotent platform.

Reasons to Not Use Puppet

- Ruby support is declining.

- Ruby-based command-line interface.

- Steep learning curve to develop custom Puppet modules.

- Code can be complex and convoluted.

- Less control than other products.

Chef

Probably one of the most widely used products for configuration management behind Puppet is Chef. Chef is a Ruby-based product like Puppet and works in a server agent architecture. Chef originally was a mixture of proprietary and open source components; however, since April 2019 Chef declared they would be open sourcing everything that is Chef. True to their work, today at the time of writing Chef has a community version of their configuration management tool available for download and use.

Ways to Use Chef

Chef currently has three ways users can use their automation platform.

Managed Service

A managed service is available from Chef for the organization or small business that does not wish to build any on-premise systems. There are additional costs involved as with any managed service.

On-Premise

For the organization that has a closed network or wishes to manage their own estate entirely from on-premise, Chef does offer the ability to download and install the infrastructure yourself. Additional costs are involved if you want support, and the pricing model has moved from price for the system to price per node managed per month.

Community

As Chef is now open source, the community open source version of Chef is available for download and use but does come with the standard warning of no support.

Reasons to Use Chef

- Nice integration with Git
- Plenty community modules and recipes available online
- Flexible
- Tools available to reduce installation complications
- State-based configuration management like Puppet

Reasons to Not Use Chef

- Ruby support is declining.

- Steep learning curve for new users.

- No push capabilities.

- Documentation has not been as good as other products.

- Enterprise support and on-premise costs can ramp up if large estates are being used.

- Not ideal for organizations with small estates.

Making the Decision

Making a decision on what automation tooling to be used can be a difficult one if you are new to automation. The following are some pointers you can use to come to the correct decision for you.

Market Trends

Looking at what the current trends are in the market or with your competitors can help you make a slightly more informed decision. I'm not advocating that you follow the herd for good or worse, I'm suggesting you look at what is working or not working for others. The market trends do not tell you how much effort has gone into setting the environment up nor does it show you the return of investment, but it does give you a better idea if one product is being used more than another. The last thing you want to do is invest time into something that will get replaced in 6–12 months.

See for Yourself

Installing and testing each platform for yourself is something I would recommend you do if you are unsure which product is right for you. My recommendation would be to take a simple use case, like building a web server. Not to install the operating system but simply just installing and starting services to turn a system into a web server. The tasks are simple and should be easily found in official documentation of each of the different products. This approach will then allow you to see how the products compare. You can then compare things like

- Documentation.

- How easy is the platform to install?

- How simple is the code to write and run?

- How steep was the learning curve to get started?

These points will help when you present your findings to your organization's holders and justify the time spent in trialing the different products.

Enterprise vs. Community vs. Cost

Do you require an enterprise product or can you use a community product? This question is normally answered within milliseconds of asking this question with some organizations, largely due to compliance regulatory requirements or other similar reasons. Whatever the reason to use whichever product, there is another very important aspect to think about.

The true cost that product will bring. This is not always the licensing or subscription cost from vendors but the cost of effort to get the platform in position to be effective for your organization. Many people are sold products by vendors based on nice examples and prebuilt use cases.

These vendors can neglect to explain the training required or the time it will take to get everything in a position to be useful. This can mislead new users in thinking the platform comes configured out of the box, almost always ending up with a platform not being used. When you spend your time testing and trialing products, ensure you factor in the effort that will be required to get your organization in a position where they can be using the product as effectively as possible.

Product Life Cycle

Road map information about a product is almost as important as the product itself. The product can offer all the greatest functionality and seem very appealing, but if the product you choose only has a short life cycle and will not have any new versions released, you are wasting your time and possibly your organization's money. Before committing to any product, ensure that the road map looks healthy.

Automation with Management Tools

To expand a bit more around using the automation tooling that is shipped with some of the various management tools, let's discuss what you can do to improve your estate management.

State Management

One very important feature you want from your automation platform or estate management tool is the ability to keep your estate's state managed. You want to configure your estate management or automation platform tool to monitor and correct any configuration drift that may occur. Whether it is by accident or through malice intent, you want to make sure that you have no nasty surprises next time there is a system reboot.

Controlling the state of all your systems will ensure your systems run exactly as they were when first built and tested. This is crucial in reducing firefighting further down the line.

Enterprise Products

Estate management tools that provide the best standard operating environment configuration capabilities are usually enterprise products unfortunately. Red Hat's "Satellite server" product or SUSE's "SUSE Manager" product is among the best choices for a Linux estate today. Both will either include Puppet or SaltStack. These products are quite good at allowing you to manage the "state" of your systems in your estate. Their implementation is quite different and will require some upskilling time. The positive thing though is the documentation is quite good, and as you are paying for the service, support is also available if you need help with anything. Most support companies will do their best to help, up to a point. Enterprise support does not mean the vendor will provide professional services for free, but they will do their best to keep you happy. In the end, you are paying for a product, and it is at their interest that you keep using it.

Use Case Example

To understand why using something is important, it often helps to see an example. Here is a basic example of a situation where a standard operating environment can prevent major issues later down the line.

The Platform Tool

In this example, we are using the Red Hat estate management tool, "Satellite server 6.x." This is the latest version of the Satellite system Red Hat is developing. This example could also make use of SaltStack if you prefer. Just adjust the naming and functionality accordingly in your mind's eye.

The Platform Tool Configuration

Red Hat Satellite 6 has the ability to configure content views with specific Puppet modules. These modules can be further enhanced with smart parameters that help manage the configuration of your estate.

In this example, a lead Linux sysadmin was smart enough to include a puppet module that controls the configuration of the estate's standard ssh_config file. This keeps the entire estate configured in such a way that no one can log in as root.

All systems in the estate are configured to run Puppet agents that check in with the Puppet master periodically.

The Mistake

Where this use case is interesting is when a simple mistake is made.

A new Linux sysadmin has been given the task of debugging a login issue on one of the preproduction systems in the estate. During the debugging process, a simple typo was accidentally entered into the ssh_config file. Unfortunately, the typo, if enforced, could cause the sshd service to fail on restart. As the Linux sysadmin is unaware of this change to the ssh_config file, they do not restart any services as they don't believe anything was changed. Why would they restart services, especially if they don't want to cause any unwanted outages, no matter how small.

Laying in the Shadows Waiting

If left unchecked, the unwanted change made by the Linux sysadmin will be applied during the next maintenance window. Usually, during these maintenance windows, updates or patches are normally applied. In most cases, a system restart would take place. As this previously undetected typo was laying in the shadows waiting, it would be at this stage that the then sleeping issue would be woken to rear its ugly head. If nothing was done to correct this problem before the system restarted, the ssh daemon would now be in a defunct state after the reboot, not allowing anyone to log in via ssh.

Safety Net

Due to the fact that the organization was smart enough to have a configuration management tool listening for unwanted configuration changes, the sysadmin's typo never matured into a problem.

The victim system's local Puppet agent checked in with the Puppet master on the Red Hat Satellite server shortly after the Linux sysadmin's typo and brought the configuration back inline with what was deemed to be the correct configuration when Puppet was configured for the environment.

If it were not for the safety net, a simple mistake like a typo could have caused a delay in any debugging for any outages that may have occurred after the problem was created. If this were a production system and an outage was extended because of sloppy work, there could have been bigger implications for the unfortunate Linux sysadmin.

Yes, this example had ways of circumventing the issue by logging in to a console, but what if this configuration was something a bit more serious like grub configuration? This would have meant the system may not have booted after its scheduled reboot, effectively creating a problem where there never should have been one in the first place.

Setting Up a SOE

To avoid issues similar to the use case explained, it is vital that the estate configuration state is managed. To have a successful SOE platform configured, you will need to make sure you have your estate management tool configured in accordance with good practices. This will require proper planning, preparation, and in some cases organization culture change.

Build from a Standard

To build your systems that will be managed by your SOE environment, you need to ensure you do the following:

- Build from a standard system build template/image or kickstart file.

- New systems should be built with all the required agents or services to register your new system to your configuration management platform.

- Ensure your systems are registered to correct environments and let the configuration management bring the configuration in line.

- Updated configuration drift to reflect configurations' current state. This way, if anything changes, you will have a log of the event.

Source Control

Any code that is being written to manage your estate should go through a proper code development process. This means the following should happen:

- All code for any automation should be stored in a source control platform such as Git.

- All code should be passed through a linting system to check basic formatting and syntax issues.

- Changes should be done via pull requests or merge requests.

- Two different people should be involved in code review.

- Code should never be pushed into a production environment without going through a staged testing process.

Phased Testing

Phased testing or staged testing is the process of testing your automation and configuration management through different environments before reaching production. The approach should be similar to the following.

Code Development

- Code developed and tested in a sandbox environment.

- A test plan for the new configuration management should be built that explains what the configuration change will look like and how it can be validated.

Code Testing and Peer Reviewed

- New code is committed to a local Git repository that has webhooks or similar into a pipeline tool that runs basic limiting or syntax testing. If the code passes its test, only then is a new merge or pull request opened for peer review.

- A second person should peer review code and approve any merge or pull requests.

Code Promotion

- Code can then be promoted into the first live testing environment. Usually, this is a development environment or similar. Remember development environments are still live as they have users on them, so caution is recommended. If possible, avoid environments that can't have downtime ideally.

- The set test plan should now be followed to ensure that nothing has been broken or caused any issues.

- If everything has worked as expected and the change has been signed off as successful, promote the code to your next environment.

Automate the Automation

Once you have your automation platform in place and you are familiar with automation practices, you will want to start evolving your practices to include more avenues of automation.

Self-Healing

Having your platform fully automated is an amazing achievement that any Linux sysadmin should be proud of. Taking the next step is what will bring your worth to your organization to a whole new level.

Building a platform that can heal itself when disaster strikes is the next major advancement all Linux sysadmins should start doing. In the past, giving your platform the ability to recognize system outages and apply solutions without you having to lift a finger is something only sci-fi movies did. Today, you can do this with an array of tools or self-developed techniques.

Self-Healing Layers

There are a few layers at which self-healing can occur. There is a hardware layer, the "platform" layer, and finally the application layer.

Each of these layers has its own areas of failure and has its own methods of recovery. If we start from the bottom up, let's look at the hardware layer.

Removing All Single Points of Failure

Hardware can be a tricky thing to self-heal if you do not have redundancy. If a physical disk or motherboard dies, no amount of automation or smart tooling is going to save you if you don't have a spare system to failover to. The first thing you always do is look at your single points of failure. For this reason, you need to have backup hardware for everything running in your estate. Sounds expensive, right? It is, but you tend to only do this level of smart estate recovery for organizations that cannot afford downtime.

Ken's Law 1   Money should not be a factor if the amount to be lost because of downtime exceeds the money for redundancy hardware.

Hardware Layer Self-Healing

Most organizations do not run on a single set of hardware devices or at least should not be. There are usually secondary or tertiary devices for failover to occur that can be used.

Where the clever bit comes is in how you recognize the hardware failure and how you switch from malfunctioning hardware to healthy hardware.

You would need clever logic that would need to pay attention to platform monitoring and logging tools. These tools can bring the attention of your self-healing platform to alerts, events, and logs. Not only should all hardware be reporting the health of its own components, hardware should also be looking for clues on how hardware closest to it is performing.

In the event of hardware failure, the self-healing system should have automated decision points to run specific actions. In the event of a completely unknown situation occurring, a fail-safe option should be triggered which could be as simple as flagging a major incident and getting a human involved. Learning from these incidents will improve your platform, so don't be disheartened while you are still perfecting the platform. It is impossible to predict every possible scenario.

The basic flow of your automation healing for your hardware should be similar to the following.

Reporting

1. Monitoring and logging systems should receive the event of hardware not checking in.

2. Estate management tools should also be notified of suspected hardware failure.

Ensuring Platform Availability

1. Failover should automatically occur to ensure there is limited or no downtime.

2. If failover fails, the process will break down into an outage. A major incident should be raised, and someone should be called out.

Automated Recovery

1. Automated recovery can start once a failover has occurred.

2. First pass of automated investigation should be triggered. That is, can any other hardware closest to the system reach the failed system?

3. If the decision has been reached that the hardware has failed, first attempt at recovery should be started. This could be accessing the API of power management that controls the hardware and doing a cold restart to see if hardware recovers.

4. After an allotted time, a second pass of investigation should be triggered to see if the failed hardware has started responding.

5. If the hardware has recovered, a full set of automated tests should be run to confirm the health of the system. If passed, the platform can fail back to the previously suspected hardware failure.

6. If hardware still remains unresponsive, the logic should make the decision to either scrap the current hardware by turning it off and provisioning a new system from spare hardware or rebuild the failed system.

    a. If a rebuild of the current system is selected, a check will need to be done to see if the defunct hardware can be reached post reboot via a network boot option. If the system can be reached from a network boot, an automated rebuild process can begin.

b. If the decision is to scrap the failed hardware, the automated self-healing platform will need to contact the power management API and boot spare hardware. A network build of an operating system will need to be done, followed by configuration as per estate configuration to bring the system back online for workload.

7. Whichever option is chosen from step 6, the recovered system will need to rejoin any clusters and mark the system as available for failback to occur.

Platform Layer Self-Healing

With the complexity of hardware self-healing, it may not be a surprise to you to know that the platform layer does tend to come with a degree of its own self-healing capabilities. "Platforms" are often either orchestration layers like OpenShift or Tanzu if you are using containers or they could be virtualization platforms like VMware or Red Hat virtualization. These platforms are designed to naturally ensure they keep workload working by allowing workload to failover from nodes that stop responding. That combined with load balancers and redundant networking should allow the platform to remain quite resilient.

That is where the self-healing mostly ends for these platforms. It is up to your clever estate self-healing logic to return the entire platform to working order. In the hardware self-healing section, we spoke about rejoining hardware to clusters. This is where your intelligent logic should come into play. Like hardware self-healing, there should be a sequence of steps that are automatically followed to ensure the platform self-heals:

1. Check for hardware availability. A record should exist of systems available for use. This is where your rebuilt system or newly built system should

report they are available for use. For those familiar with OpenStack, this is like a bare metal server list reporting its availability state.

2. Remove failed system. Systems that were marked as dead should be removed from clusters and have any cleanup work completed before the new hardware is added.

3. Add to cluster. The available system should then be configured as a new node or host. The configuration should include adding the system to the cluster and testing a workload. Provided all passed, workload can be scheduled back on the node or host.

Application Layer Self-Healing

Application self-healing should be down to the application server that hosts the application generally, but if you were to think more about the inner workings of the application, additional self-healing could be done.

Improving the application data health or connectivity to databases could be controlled with automation. If a database server became unavailable, rebuilds could occur and databases replicated. There are a fair number of things that can be done, but ideally if your application is simple enough, all that would be required would be to redeploy and redirect traffic.

For more complex applications, developers would need to build in functionality for applications to recover from failure. This subject is best left for the developers.

When to Self-Heal

Building your automation and self-healing platform should be based on when you want self-healing to occur. Do you want to pay attention only when a failure has occurred, or do you want to watch for signs that a problem is immanent?

Do you want to be proactive or reactive?

I'm sure you can agree that it is much better to catch a problem before it can become a bigger issue later on. By being proactive, you can then have your self-healing system resolve issues in a less intrusive manner. This could allow your system or systems to properly shut down and rebuild. Failovers can then be scheduled when traffic has decreased, and nodes can then be drained gracefully instead of forcefully. By allowing rebuilds to occur in a controlled manner, outages can be scheduled to accommodate organizational processes like proper change control. With this flow, everything can be automated including the admin work to get platform change approval.

How to Implement Self-Healing

Talking about self-healing in theory is simple enough, but how do you go about implementing a solution like this for your estate? To fully discuss self-healing techniques and do it proper justice, we would definitely require another full book. However, let's look lightly into how you may get started with a few breadcrumbs for you to further investigate.

Gates

Just like you need gates to control the water flow in a canal, you will need gates to control your self-healing environments. These gates should be stop points to validate what has just happened. You wouldn't want to start a lengthy process of remediation if a simple solution was not checked first. That is, has a reboot worked?

Gates don't have to be technical configuration either. A highly regulated organization may not want clever logic going around rebuilding systems without being approved. For this, you could introduce a change control gate. A proactive self-healing platform could identify a potential problem and raise a change request. If the change request is approved, the remediation actions would then continue, within a regulated change window.

Another useful gate could be to pause after a failed system has been rebuilt before failing traffic back over to it, in case an underlying issue has not been detected.

Gates in general should be the first things you build when developing your self-healing platform. Think of them as diagnostic stops while you are proving your logic works.

Tooling: Automation and State Management

Using a combination of state management tools and automation platforms, you should be more than capable of stringing together enough logic to do some interesting self-healing. You will need to work out how to parse logs for important information. Having a log gathering system like Splunk that is constantly being scraped would allow you to build a database of potential issues. If your self-healing logic matches anything that could be a problem, you could then report an issue to a message bus. Another big part of your self-healing estate could then monitor the message bus for different kinds of jobs that would need self-healing jobs run.

Configuration and applications running together could quickly get overly complex. Take enough time and design your approach before you start building to see if this is the best option for you.

Machine Learning

Another way of developing your own self-healing platform could be done by teaching it to understand what to do under certain conditions. For this, you need to build a neural network of scenarios. That could include looking at logs, alerts, and events. Your self-healing logic should then weigh the percentage of data that is matched to a condition that will trigger a sequence of automation tasks. Tasks can then be run from estate management tools and automation platforms. Most of the tools available today also have the ability to integrate with service desk platforms to raise incidents and even have the capability to initiate communication with a standby engineer.

Machine learning though is a steep learning curve and requires a certain aptitude to master. If it is something you are interested in, spend some time playing with a few basic examples and take it from there. The Internet is a great place to learn from and is full of people with nice examples you can try.

One important note about starting with machine learning is that you will need some hefty number crunching hardware to compile your machine learning programs. If you are fortunate to have a decent GPU, you could start with that. Adding more GPUs will decrease your compilation time, but with the general shortage of GPUs today, you could face an uphill struggle with this one.

Tip Don't be afraid of secondhand hardware; using someone else's unloved older hardware may still help you when you are getting started and will save you some money too.

Off-the-Shelf Products

If you have the budget and don't have the time or patience to build your own platform, you could look at some of the "off-the-shelf" options.

These products can provide a fair bit of functionality but may not give you everything you may need. Pay close attention to what is included out of the box and what you need to configure yourself. It could be a glorified automation engine that still requires you to write logic, or worse. Buy some of the organization's professional services to build the logic for you.

Dynatrace

One product I have heard about in the past is Dynatrace. I know very little about the product as I have never used it before and am not making any recommendations based on what I know, so I will leave it up to you to research and check for yourself. I only remember Dynatrace because I attended a presentation at Red Hat Summit in Boston a couple years back.

During the presentation, the presenter explained how they used Dynatrace to manage their own estate, and while the presentation was happening, there was an outage with one of their web servers (possibly staged for effect). The Dynatrace platform basically kicked in and started running its diagnostics and potential remediation work. It did however notify the presenter there was a problem, which I guess any monitoring platform could do anyways.

The impression I got though was that Dynatrace could do some smart things and could potentially be a good option. Like I mentioned, do your own checking and testing before jumping in with both feet.

Automation Best Practices

There is ultimately no list of all the best practices you can follow when it comes to automating your estate. The best advice in this regard would be to understand all the best practices for the automation platform you decide to use. Get familiar with configuration file locations and how they should be configured.

Do Not Reinvent the Wheel, Again …

This is an area many people fail in, and I'm sure you are getting tired of me mentioning it as I have spoken about this now at least a few times. It's something too many people keep doing, including myself, so by mentioning it all the time I'm hoping by the end of this book, it would be so drilled into you that you never try to reinvent anything again.

Always avoid trying to develop everything from scratch, especially if you can get something similar if not identical to what you want online. There really is no reason to spend time on something that already exists. By all means, take the code and adjust it to fit what you want to do, but do not just develop from the beginning every time. I do understand there will be times when writing a role or puppet module might be quicker, but always ask yourself honestly.

"How long will this take to write?"

If the answer is longer than five minutes, you know you are then spending time where you may not need to. You are better off spending that extra time testing and perfecting your platform configuration.

Code Libraries

Most if not all major automation platforms have vast libraries of online examples and code you can download. If your first step is to make a decision on which automation platform to use, your next step should be to find the equivalent online library of code or modules.

149

Ansible

In the Ansible world, you can make use of the Ansible Galaxy. The Ansible Galaxy has a vast array of different Ansible roles you can search for and use by the tags people have associated with them.

```
https://galaxy.ansible.com/
```

Puppet

Like Ansible, Puppet has a great library similar to Ansible Galaxy called Puppet Forge.

```
https://forge.puppet.com/
```

SaltStack

SaltStack doesn't quite have the same setup but does have a GitHub location called SaltStack formulas with tons of content.

```
https://github.com/saltstack-formulas
```

Note   Ansible is my personal choice; this is why I use it as an example quite often. I try not to recommend anything directly as I want to avoid being biased toward one particular vendor or product. Always make your own decision based on an informed opinion.

Metadata

Once you get yourself in a position to contribute code back to the community you have chosen to follow, make sure you understand how to format and build your code so the correct metadata can be used to catalog your work. Nothing is more frustrating than providing code that no one can find or use.

Using examples from your chosen provider can help get you started. Download an example and "borrow" the code from there.

Things to Avoid

A few things to avoid when automating, no matter what platform you decide to use.

Shell Scripts

If possible, use modules and code provided by your automation tool of choice. Ansible as an example has a rich library of Ansible modules available. Not everything is installed by default anymore but can be installed with Ansible collections. Similar approaches may be available with other platforms. Always investigate what the best way to run a task is before you resort to a shell script.

Shell scripts tend to be non-idempotent and would require further code to ensure they were. Using a prebuilt module that speaks to a platform API or similar would handle all the extra coding for you and leave you with neat clean code.

Restarting Services When Not Required

If your automation code has a service restart task, never restart just for the sake of restarting. Use control code that checks if the service actually needs to be restarted. Even though it could be a slight dip in service, it poses a risk if configuration is not correct. Some services could refuse to start, and you end up with an outage.

Using Old Versions

Seems obvious, but make sure you are using the latest possible version of the automation tool you have chosen. Documentation may not always update if code you are writing is going to be deprecated.

Correct Version Documentation

Read the latest documentation or at least the documentation that matches the version of the automation tool you are using. Code changes and modules become deprecated, so following old examples or old knowledge base articles can set you back when you need to refactor your code later down the line.

Good Practices

As there are things you should always avoid when writing automation code, there are also a few good practices you should include in your working methods.

Debugging

Remember to remove extra debugging steps or tasks added to your code. It may be useful when you are testing and developing your code but can look untidy when used in production. It could also get you some unwanted questions from people who do not understand why there are red lines everywhere when they execute your automation tasks.

Don't Forget README

Documenting your code for others to use is very important when you are not working alone. The whole point of automation is saving time; spending that time explaining to others how to use your code is counterintuitive.

It is also well recommended when you are sharing code online through different sharing portals. Getting used to doing it when you start is the best way to continue doing it.

Source Control

Commit your code to GitHub/GitLab or whichever git provider you prefer, but do it often and always before you stop for the day. Not only is your code safe but also allows you to build a portfolio of your work for others to use.

Summary

In this chapter, we discussed the following:

- The theory points around automation, when to automate and when not to.

- What it means to develop code that is idempotent.

- Various automation platforms available today. Why you would use them and why you would not use them.

- What standard operating environments are and how you could configure your estate to be one.

- How hardware, system platforms, and applications could be configured to self-heal.

- Automation best practices and things that should be avoided.

CHAPTER 6

Containers

This chapter goes in a slightly different direction from previous chapters. This will be the first chapter where we discuss organization workload and how to manage that workload. Previously, we discussed platforms, automation, and general Linux system administration. We will touch a bit more on platforms toward the end of this chapter but will be more structured around the major topic of this chapter: containers.

This chapter will delve into the world of containerization and how you can manage workloads within them. We will discuss what containers are, how you can get started with them, what you should be doing to manage them, and the dos and don'ts. Finally, we will end the chapter on how you can manage a full estate of containers using tools available today.

The goal of this chapter is to help you get a basic understanding of containers and the orchestration tools you can use to manage them.

Getting Started

As a Linux sysadmin, you have most likely already heard of containers; you may already be using them in your organization.

Containers are the next major evolution in Linux estates. It is important that as a Linux sysadmin you are fully aware of what they are, how they are built, and, most importantly, how they are managed.

Simply put, a container is a set of one or more processes and files managed within its own isolated environment.

© Kenneth Hitchcock 2022
K. Hitchcock, *Linux System Administration for the 2020s*,
https://doi.org/10.1007/978-1-4842-7984-7_6

Virtual Machine vs. Container

Where a virtual machine is a complete operating system with its own files and resources, a container is an isolated part of an operating system that not only has its own binaries and files but also shares libraries and binaries with its host operating system. Containers are created and run on top of a system layer known as a container runtime (Figure 6-1).

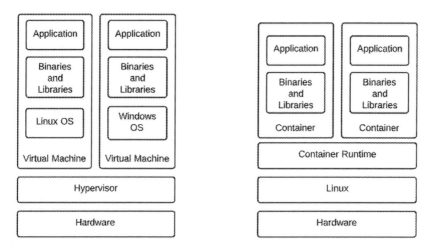

Figure 6-1. *demonstrates the different layers required for virtual machines and containers*

The differences between a virtual machine and a container are shown in Figure 6-1.

Container History

The idea of a container is not a new concept at all and as a concept has been around longer than Linux itself. Containers started their conceptual journey in the late 1970s and early 1980s with the first introduction of using chroot to create isolated environments. Later in the early 2000s, Solaris and FreeBSD expanded the idea with practical implementations of platforms that provided segregation.

It was not until Google later introduced the ability to separate resources like CPU and memory by introducing Cgroups that the world of containers really started to grow. With the concept of Cgroups, the likes of LXC (Linux containers) and systemd-nspawn could create their own early forms of containers. LXC looked at creating full system containers where systemd-nspawn could manage namespaced processes and be controlled by systemd. Both were the early leaders in containers. Docker based much of their early development using LXC but later dropped LXC in favor of starting a container standard. This was the birth of the Open Container Initiative (OCI) and became the standard for all container runtimes.

There are a number of container runtimes that can be used today to create containers, largely due to the fact that all container runtimes follow this standard.

Container Runtimes

Container runtimes are what makes it possible to run a container on your system. A container runtime allows the container to speak to the host kernel and run processes.

The original container runtimes were simple and could run in isolated environments, but over time these runtimes have become more complex and have evolved where multiple layers are required to manage containers in complex environments. For you to understand the full flow of how containers are created and managed today, there are three categories you need to understand about container runtimes:

- Low-level runtimes or OCI runtimes

- Container runtime interfaces

- Container engines

Low-Level or OCI Runtimes

At the lowest level when using containers are the OCI runtimes. OCI runtimes focus mainly on the container life cycle. This is the basic creation and running of containers.

Low-level runtimes have two variations, native and "virtualized."

Native Runtimes

Native OCI runtimes run their processes on the same kernel of the host system where the OCI runtime is running.

Note   Due to the fact that the host shares its kernel with the native runtime, there is a concern that a compromised container could impact the host it is running on. For this reason, you should always understand all the security issues that you could potentially be building into your containers.

Some examples of native OCI runtimes are runc, crun, and containerd.

Virtual and Sandboxed Runtimes

Unlike native runtimes, virtual and sandboxed runtimes are more isolated from the host kernel.

Sandbox Runtimes

Sandbox runtimes create a proxy layer referred to as a unikernel which proxies requests to the host kernel, reducing possible issues if a container were ever compromised. Sandbox runtimes available as of writing are gVisor and nabla-containers.

Virtual Runtimes

Instead of using a proxy layer, virtual runtimes create a virtual machine to use instead of the host kernel. These runtimes can be slower but provide another strong layer of protection. Virtual runtimes available as of writing are Katacontainers, Sysbox, and Firecracker-containerd, to name a few.

Container Runtime Interface

With the growth of container workloads and the evolution of tools like Kubernetes, there became a need to move away from hardcoded runtimes that were built into the kubelet daemons. The idea was to create a new interface that allowed tools like Kubernetes to speak to any container runtimes without needing to recompile kubelets each time a new runtime was used. This new interfacing allowed greater flexibility to switch out native runtimes.

A CRI needs to be able to do the following:

- Start and stop pods

- Manage start, stop, and kill type operations within a pod

- Pull and push images from container registries

- Assist in metric and log retrieval

There are two main CRI options today that are capable of doing the preceding steps. They are containerd and CRI-O.

Containerd

A high-level runtime developed by Docker with runc under the covers, Containerd contains all the functionality of a CRI and is regarded as a good example of a CRI.

CRI-O

CRI-O is a slimmer implementation of a CRI. Red Hat is currently supporting the integration of CRI-O into Kubernetes and their OpenShift product. Docker was removed in favor of moving to a CRI type architecture, thus enabling the flexibility of switching low-level runtimes.

Container Engines

The final category of container runtimes you need to understand is the layer where you can actually do some container creation. This layer is the container engine. Just like a virtual machine requires a hypervisor to run on, containers require a container engine.

From the diagram in the "Virtual Machine vs. Container" section, you can see where the container engine layer exists between containers and the operating system. This is the container engine.

Table 6-1 lists the two common container engines that are used today; they are Docker and Podman. Throughout this chapter, we will be using Podman as the container engine for any container examples or exercises.

Table 6-1. *Container engine examples*

Tool Name	Description
Docker	Released in March of 2013. One of the first mass used container runtimes
Podman	Unlike Docker, Podman does not run an underlying daemon to run containers

Docker

Today when I speak to people about containers, they often still refer to containers as "Docker containers." Docker was the first real container engine most people used; many still use Docker and still swear by it.

If you are a Docker or Podman person, it does not matter too much if you are just using it on your laptop or test lab; in the end, all you want to do is create a container based on an image.

Docker, however, has become a bit more difficult to install since I first used it. In the past, the Docker binaries could be installed with dnf or yum, but now you may need to have separate repositories enabled or have special subscriptions. If Docker is the choice you wish to go with, you will need to read the documentation.

I have managed to install "Docker" on my Fedora system using the following command:

```
# dnf install docker -y
```

Once Docker has been installed, you may want to read the man pages on how Docker is used.

You will need to understand how to start a container, find out if the container is running, and how to delete the container when you are done. Table 6-2 lists some of the docker parameter options that can be used.

Table 6-2. Docker example options from Docker help

Tool Name	Description
start	Start one or more stopped containers
stop	Stop a container
ps	List running containers
attach	Attach local standard input, output, and error streams to a running container
search	Search the Docker registries for a container image
history	Show the history of an image
images	Show all the images that have been pulled to your local system
create	Create a new container
build	Build an image from a Dockerfile
events	Get real-time events from the server
kill	Kill one or more running containers
rmi	Remove container image

Podman

Podman came a while after Docker and is similar to Docker in how containers are created and managed. One major difference between Podman and Docker is that Podman does not require a service or daemon to be running. This is due to the fact that Docker runs on top of a runc container, whereas Podman does not. Instead, Podman directly uses runc containers.

All Docker commands should work with Podman; the help and man pages from Podman will also be a great source of information when you are starting.

Podman and Docker can use the same images and Dockerfiles, so if you find any Docker examples they should work with Podman too.

Installing Podman is as simple as running your install command for your local package management system. In the case of Fedora, the command to install Podman is

```
# dnf install podman -y
```

To check the man pages for Podman, you can run

```
# man podman
```

If the man pages are too long to read and you just want to get started, run

```
# podman help
```

Similar to Docker, you can search for images, and you can list local images and containers. If you have any Dockerfiles, you can use those to build custom images if you like, and most importantly you can create containers.

Podman is simple enough to get your head around, and there are plenty of examples for both Podman and Docker online.

If you are not familiar with either Docker or Podman, do not worry too much. We will be running through some practical examples for you to try shortly.

Container Images

If you were to build a virtual machine, you would need to create a "virtual machine shell" in your hypervisor, boot the virtual machine, and install an operating system. Containers, as they share libraries with the operating system, typically do not need their own operating system installed. Instead, container images are created with the files and libraries required for the container to run its workload.

An example could be a container image that is going to be used as a nginx web server. The basic configuration and libraries will need to be installed within the image as not all hosts that will run container runtimes would have nginx installed. The same can be said for any application server binaries that may be required.

It's this ability to ship the binaries and files for an application that really allows containers to be completely portable. More on that further in this chapter.

Container Registries

You can imagine that container image variations could grow quite large; just by thinking of a few examples alone, you can see the number growing. For that reason, it is important to store these images for later use. No one will want to create a new image each time they have a particular workload they wish to deploy. If you have had any experience building application servers, you will understand that some configuration can be quite time consuming. Having to repeat the configuration process for each new environment is not something I would recommend.

This is where container registries become useful; they not only store the custom images that you create for your organization but also the libraries of downloaded images for particular workloads you may have. Instead of building a php image, for example, you could find a php container image with everything available to run your php application.

Container registries are available to you in a few ways. There are cloud or Internet registries where you can pull images you may need. You can then customize these images and push them to your private cloud repositories if you choose, or you can push them to your local on-premise registries.

Cloud Registries

Cloud registries are a great way to work with images if you have a small estate to manage. Just like it does not make sense to build an estate management platform for a small number of systems in your estate, the same is true for a small container estate. If all you are using containers for is some basic applications that do not change often, hosting your images in a cloud registry makes perfect sense.

Companies like IBM and Google have cloud registry options for you to host your container images. Depending on your organization requirements, Google could be a good place to start. They offer a $300 free tier for testing Google services which include registry options. After the trial is finished, there will of course be a cost involved; just like evaluating estate management tools, you will need to work out what works best for you.

Local Registries

If you have a deeper requirement for container image storage, you may want to consider looking at on-premise container registry options. The options available will drastically depend on the level of service you will need. This could be as simple as just having a place to store container images in a disconnected or air-gapped environment, or it could be more complex in that you require image scanning for security reasons. Whatever your requirements, trial and test to confirm what works for you.

Container Registry Providers

There are a number of options you can choose if you need a container registry. Just like most things we have discussed so far in this book, there are community products, and there are enterprise products.

With community products, you get basic functionality and in most cases quite nice features. With enterprise products, you gain all the goodness around security and compliance scanning.

When choosing, you will need to consider everything again from price to features.

Containers in Practice

Now with the basics of containers covered in theory, let's get some hands-on experience with creating container workloads.

Prerequisites

For this section of the book, you will need to have the following available to you if you wish to test some of the configuration that will be discussed.

Shopping List

- A Linux system with root privileges

- Access to the Internet from the Linux system

- Ability to install packages

System Prep

Before we can create any of the containers or configurations, you need to prep the system you will be using.

Install Packages

Install the Podman, Docker, or whichever runtime packages using the official documentation if you are not familiar with the process. In most cases, this will be as simple as running "dnf install podman -y" or "apt-get -y install podman".

The Docker installation may be a bit different from Podman as you may need to enable extra repositories to get the required packages. Check the official documentation to be sure.

Note   For this section, I will be using Podman; for that reason, it may be worth using Podman to avoid extra config or google searching.

Creating Containers

Over the next few pages, we will cover the basic hands-on experience you will need to start working with basic containers. The goal for this section is not to make you a container specialist but more to show you how to create a simple container environment to gain experience with.

Warning   The following exercises are not meant to be used for production or live environments. They are not resilient enough and would cause you more problems than what they are worth. For production type environments, you will need to look more at container orchestration tooling.

Pulling a Container Image

Before a container can be created or run, you will need to pull a base image from a cloud registry or, if you are ahead of the curve, from a local registry.

To pull the correct image from a registry, you should know what the container workload will run. Is the container going to be a nginx server? Are you going to run a php application? Or do you have something entirely different in mind?

Finding Container Images

Once you know what type of container you will run, you can search for a container image that closely resembles your intended workload. If you wanted to find a nginx image to run a basic web server container, you would run something similar to the following:

```
#podman search nginx
```

The output would list all the available images that contain the nginx keyword. Pay attention to the number of stars and if the image is from an official source:

```
INDEX      NAME                        DESCRIPTION
  STARS  OFFICIAL
docker.io  docker.io/library/nginx  Official build of Nginx.
  15732  [OK]
...output reduced
```

Pulling the Container Image

From the list of available container images you discovered with the podman search command, you can now pull or download the image to your local system. It is this process that will allow you to use the image locally for any containers you wish to run.

To pull a container image from the previous search command, you can use a command very similar to the following:

```
# podman pull docker.io/library/nginx
```

The output should look similar to the following:

```
#root@localhost ~]# podman pull docker.io/library/nginx
Trying to pull docker.io/library/nginx:latest...
Getting image source signatures
```

```
Copying blob fca7e12d1754 [==============>-------] 20.6MiB / 25.4MiB
Copying blob 858292fd2e56 done
Copying blob 1c84ebdff681 done
Copying blob a4723e260b6f done
Copying blob b380bbd43752 done
Copying blob 745ab57616cb done
```

Container images can be downloaded as archive files if you need to save them to a portable storage device for another system.

Local Container Images

To see what container images you have downloaded, you can run a command similar to the following. These images can be used to create containers on your local system.

```
# podman images
```

The output should be similar to the following:

```
[root@localhost ~]# podman images
REPOSITORY                  TAG        IMAGE ID
  CREATED        SIZE
docker.io/library/nginx     latest     87a94228f133
  3 weeks ago    138 MB
```

Running a Container

If you found the container image you wish to use and have managed to download or pull it successfully, you can run a basic container instance of that image on your test system. To run a basic nginx container from the previously downloaded nginx image, you run a command similar to the following:

```
[root@localhost ~]# podman run -d --name kentest -p 8080:80 nginx
```

The output would be the ID of the container that gets created:

95bf289585a8caef7e9b9ae6bac0918e99aaac64d46b461180484c8dd1efa0a4

The "-d" option in the command tells podman to detach from the running container and leave it to run in the background. The "-p" sets the port that the container will listen on.

Running Containers

Once you have created your container, you may want to see if it is running. The simplest way of doing this is to run a container list command as per the following:

```
[root@localhost ~]# podman container list
CONTAINER ID   IMAGE     COMMAND     CREATED   STATUS
PORTS                    NAMES
95bf289585a8  dock....  nginx...  7 sec...    Up
0.0.0.0:8080->80/tcp kentest
```

From the list, you can see all the containers you have managed to start on your local system. The nginx example is running on all interfaces and listening on port 8080.

Welcome to nginx!

If you see this page, the nginx web server is successfully installed and working. Further configuration is required.

For online documentation and support please refer to nginx.org.
Commercial support is available at nginx.com.

Thank you for using nginx.

Figure 6-2.

The screenshot in Figure 6-2 shows the nginx serving requests on the localhost on port 8080.

Custom Images and Containers

Now that we know how to download and run basic containers from online image registries, we can explore how to customize an image to host your own workload.

Create a Podman Image Registry

The custom images created in the next few sections will need to be stored in a local registry. Without having to purchase or pay for any online service to act as a container registry, we can set up one on your local system. For this, we will create a basic podman registry and push our new images to the local container run registry.

Create a Directory for Data to Be Stored

```
# mkdir -p /var/lib/registry
```

Create Registry Container

The command to create the running container is as follows; included in the command is a "-v" parameter, which tells the container to mount a directory from the host system to the running container. In this case, this is there to help the container registry retain container images when the container is restarted.

```
# podman run --privileged -d --name registry -p 5000:5000 -v /
var/lib/registry:/var/lib/registry --restart=always registry:2
```

Set Podman to Use Insecure Registry

As container registries normally want to be secured, you need to tell podman to use an insecure registry. You can configure your registry to use a signed certificate, but for that you should follow the podman documentation.

To set podman to use an insecure registry, you will need to edit the "/etc/containers/registries.conf" file and find the "[registries.insecure]" section. Under the "[registries.insecure]" section, find the line "registries = [ ]" and update it to "registries = ['localhost:5000']".

Finally, after saving the registries.conf file, you will need to restart the podman service:

```
# systemctl restart podman
```

Using the Podman Registry

Now with your own local podman registry configured from the previous section, you are now able to add your own images to it for safekeeping. You can then pull images from your own registry when building new applications or images.

Tagging Images

The first thing you will need to do when you have local images downloaded is to tag them with your internal podman registry. This way, you can instruct podman to push images to the local registry instead of a remote registry. Think of it as a way to change the path of a container image.

To tag an image, you run the podman tag command. If we take the example of nginx that we have been using so far, we can tag the nginx image with the following command:

```
# podman tag docker.io/library/nginx localhost:5000/nginx
```

Pushing Images

With the nginx image tagged, the next step is to push or upload the nginx image to the local repository. This can be done with the following command:

```
# podman push localhost:5000/nginx
```

Remote Registries

If you created a podman registry on a different host and exposed the registry on the network interface instead of the loopback address, you can tag and push your images to that address too if you wish. Just be sure to open any firewall ports to allow traffic through to the podman registry.

The same can be said for any on-premise image registry; as long as you have the ability and permissions to push images, the podman tagging and push commands will allow you to use local registries.

Customize an Image

So far, all we have done is use container images as they are without adding any of our own customizations.

What good would a web server be without any content, right? The same can be said for container images; what's the point of running a nginx or apache web server if you don't host any web content on them?

Let's have a look at how to add our own custom content to a web server.

Dockerfile

To understand how to add some basic customizations to a container image, we will need to use a build file. This build file is most commonly referred to as a Dockerfile. Both Podman and Docker can use Dockerfiles.

These Dockerfiles are used to create any customizations you would like in your container image. Think of these files as image install files.

To use a Dockerfile, all you need to do is create a new file called Dockerfile. Do not change the name or add any extensions. The file needs to exist in the current directory, or you need to specify the location when you run the podman build command.

Example

Like before, let's run through an example. For this example, we are going to build a CentOS image with apache httpd installed on it. Once the web server packages are installed, the example will pull down an example HTML file from my GitHub account. Finally, we will run a new container with the new image.

Pull Down CentOS Image

Before we start, you will need to pull down a version of CentOS:

```
# podman pull docker.io/library/centos
```

Dockerfile

Next, you will need to create a Dockerfile. Remember that the Dockerfile should be named exactly as "Dockerfile." Ensure that you are in the same directory as your Dockerfile when you try to build your new image.

The Dockerfile in my example will pull the latest CentOS image it can find if you have not already pulled one. Once the image is available, yum will install both the "httpd" and "git" packages. These will make up all the packages required for our custom image. Feel free to add anything else you want to use like PHP. Once the packages are installed, a git clone will pull down the source code for our web content and move it to the /var/www/ html directory for the web server to use. In this example, I wrote a very basic HTML page. This can be anything you wish, so change with your own content if you want to try something a bit different.

The following is what the Dockerfile I used looks like:

```
FROM centos:latest
RUN yum -y install httpd git; \
git clone https://github.com/kenhitchcock/basicwebapp.git; \
mv basicwebapp/index.html /var/www/html/index.html
CMD ["/usr/sbin/httpd", "-D", "FOREGROUND"]
EXPOSE 80
```

Build Image

To build the image based on our earlier Dockerfile , you need to ensure you are in the same directory as your Dockerfile, then run the podman build command:

```
# podman build -t centos .
```

Note   The "." tells the podman command to use the current directory. This is why you need to be in the same directory as the Dockerfile when you run the build command. The name of the image built can be anything you want, just change the text after the "-t" parameter. This example uses the CentOS name.

Create Container

With the newly built container image and the custom content, we can run and test the new image:

```
# podman run  -p 80:80 -dit localhost/centos
```

> **Challenge**   The default port for the apache web server is 80. As a challenge, try and find out how to customize your Dockerfile to use a different port.

Confirm Container Is Running

To double-check that your container has actually started, you can run the following command:

```
# podman ps
```

The output should be similar to the following:

```
# podman ps
CONTAINER ID    IMAGE                         COMMAND
CREATED         STATUS          PORTS          NAMES
08832f29f46e    localhost/centos:latest    /usr/sbin/httpd -...
24 hours ago    Up 12 minutes ago    0.0.0.0:80->80/tcp    elated_jepsen
```

Delete Container

To delete a container, you first need to stop the container, and then you can delete it. This can be done with similar commands to the following:

```
# podman stop 08832f29f46e
# podman rm 08832f29f46e
```

The output should be similar to

```
# podman rm 08832f29f46e
08832f29f46edab6bdd41227a542bf494f926831d099a0a83ee8838bfe71fdf9
```

Container Practices

With a better understanding of what containers are and how to manage them, you now need to understand what constitutes good and bad practices.

Cloud Native

The first thing you need to understand when working with containerized workloads is what cloud native means.

The simplest explanation of cloud native is that it is the practice of using cloud technologies to deploy workloads in a lightweight and fast manner.

Cloud-native tools typically involve using automation, scalable platforms in private or public clouds, containers, service meshes, and generally with immutable infrastructure. The use of these tools and many others can enable high rates of product workload releases. Netflix is an excellent example of this. Netflix releases around 100 production releases in a day through lightweight, fast workloads that are streamlined to production by using automation and other tooling.

Good Practices

Keep It Small

The number one rule to running any container or cloud-native workload is to keep the workload as small as possible. It is not recommended to create workloads that are in the gigabyte size range. The smaller the workload, the better for deployment and scalability. If your workload demands higher sizing, then potentially you need to rearchitect how the workload is written. This could be breaking the workload down into microservices and working from there.

Always push back if you are forced to create large workload deployments. The benefits of running smaller workloads will pay off in the long term.

Dynamic Deployment

Workload deployment should never be done manually. Code should be committed to your source control and pushed through to production. Make use of pipelining tools, source control webhooks, and anything else that can trigger workload deployment.

A basic example of what this should look like can be seen in Figure 6-3.

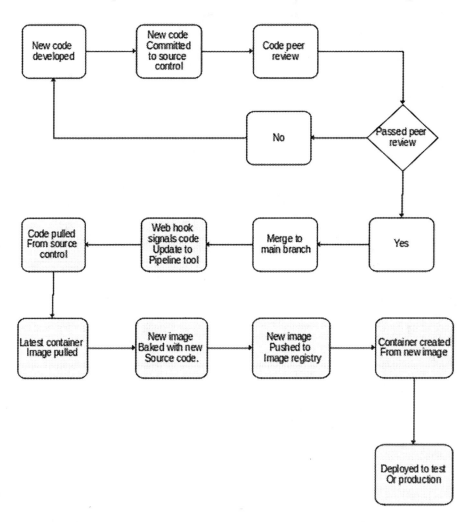

Figure 6-3.

Scalable

Any workload or application that will be deployed in a cloud type environment or be considered cloud native must be scalable. The ability to scale up when demand increases is vital to good cloud working practices. If the workload you are deploying cannot scale dynamically, you need to consider rearchitecting the workload. Not being able to scale dynamically is symptomatic of dated workloads and potentially old code.

"Does It Cloud"?

Just because you are deploying into a cloud platform does not mean your workload is cloud native. There are many other things that make workloads cloud native, but the three questions you should ask when you want to know if your workload is for the cloud are

- Is the workload small?

- Can the workload be scaled?

- Can the workload be dynamically deployed?

With the preceding questions, you can now ask yourself, "does it cloud"? If your answer is no to any of the questions, you have work to do before you can migrate or deploy to a cloud environment effectively.

Do not fall into the trap by trying to build virtual machines into containers or into cloud-native style hyperscalers. Just because you can does not always mean you should. The pitfalls to doing this will come back to bite you later on when you are not able to take advantage of the benefits of cloud computing. Large workloads can be inefficient and wasteful, negating the cost saving you may have been expecting.

If you need big workloads, then container or cloud platforms may not be what you need right now. Take a step back and look carefully at the workload first, refactor code, and break monoliths down into smaller applications that can "cloud" as the cloud was intended.

Bad Practices

There are many good practices and many bad practices. These are referred to as antipatterns. Here are a couple more common practices that should be avoided when possible.

Containers Are Not Virtual Machines

Containers are not the same as virtual machines and should not be treated the same. A container is a cutdown entity that has one purpose. This practice ensures cloud principles stay intact. If you are trying to replicate what a virtual machine does, then you may not be ready to use containers yet.

Different Images

The temptation can be to use different images for different environments, as it seems like a more secure method of building workload images. However, building test images for test, development images for development, and production images for production opens the possibility for differences to occur that are not tested and signed off. It is very possible that an image used in your test environment could have no vulnerabilities, but an image used in production does. For this reason, migrate the application-baked images through your environments. This way, you ensure security checks are done, and code is properly tested and most importantly signed off for production use (Figure 6-4).

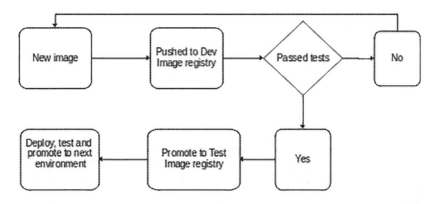

Figure 6-4.

The basic idea on how images are tested and promoted should be similar to Figure 6-4.

Production Builds from Code

This point is similar to the previous one. Do not bake your container images directly into production. Your images should be built in development and then promoted through your different staging environments. You could end up with a situation where different code is deployed to different systems. Having a single entry point into your production environment from a central image registry will greatly reduce the risk of this happening. You are also then assured that the code tested is the code deployed.

Hardcoded Secrets or Configuration

Applications should be agnostic of platform configuration or secrets. The need to hardcode anything should be an alarm bell that the application is not cloud native. Configuration and secrets should be managed by the platform the application will be deployed on; anything else is generally regarded as a bad practice and a potential security risk.

Building Idempotent Containers

Building a container should be an idempotent process. Your Dockerfiles should not be trying to make changes external to the image it is building. There should not be any code being committed or any external changes being pushed. Simply put, a container build should follow a flow similar to Figure 6-5.

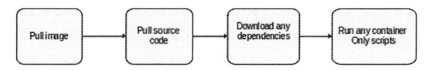

Figure 6-5.

Building container images should only focus on what is required for the container to run. The flow should be as simple as what is shown in Figure 6-5.

Container Development

In this chapter so far, we have touched briefly on how containers can be developed. We have explored some simple good and bad practices and hopefully given you a good idea what cloud native is. For this section, let's understand how you can create a meaningful workload using container development.

Development Considerations

Coding Languages

Writing code for containers is no different than writing code for your local development environment or laptop. You can still choose and use your favorite development language and can still push code to your favorite source control platform. There is no hard and fast rule that says you cannot use one particular language or the other. However, not all development languages are created equally. Using older languages may not translate to the cloud as effectively as newer ones. Before starting to write any new application, spend some time looking at some of the following options. Table 6-3 lists a few development language options that are used today within containerized applications.

Table 6-3. *Development languages or frameworks*

Language Name	Description
Quarkus	API Java framework optimized for cloud environments
React	Java framework for UI development
Python, Ruby	General-purpose high-level programming languages
Golang	Fast and robust, often used for IoT devices
.Net	If you need to stick to Microsoft-based languages

Code Editor

To write useful code, you need to practice and have an editor that works well enough without breaking the bank. There are a few available you can use, but it always comes down to personal preference and what features you are willing to live without. Table 6-4 lists a few code editor options that can be used.

Table 6-4. *Code editors*

Tool Name	Description
VSCode	Free to use, simple to understand, and has a great selection of plugins and add-ons
Eclipse	Great editor with the ability to add application servers for code testing. Generally a Java developer tool
NetBeans	Another Java editor
Notepad++	More advanced than your standard text editors, a useful option when you have limited choices
Vim	Not always installed on Linux systems but can be used to develop code. Plugins can be installed but tend to be more limited than GUI options
Nano, Emacs	More command-line editors can be used, but can lack the rich features a GUI tool can offer

Tip   VSCode is free to use, has great plugins, and is quite simple to use. Before you spend too much time with other editors, try VSCode and change if you find something better.

Source Control

No matter which source control platform you wish to use, just make sure you use one. Not using source control is a massive mistake for any developer or organization. You lose the ability to peer review code in an effective centralized manner, and you risk the loss of code. It is not worth taking the risk. Table 6-5 lists source control options that can be used to control your source code.

Table 6-5. *Source control options*

Tool Name	Description
Git	Basic git can be deployed on any Linux system; code can be pushed and pulled
GitHub	Internet-based Git source control platform
GitLab	Similar to GitHub, except you can run your own GitLab on-premise
Bitbucket	Another Git product that can be run on-premise
Subversion	Popular option prior to Git and currently losing popularity
Mercurial	Handles projects of all sizes, a free distributed control management service
Microsoft Team Foundation Server	Source control system developed by Microsoft

Note   Git is probably the most popular source control system today. Get familiar with it asap.

Container Tooling

Once you have your code developed and container ideas in place, you will want to start working on streamlining your container image creation. There are many ways to do this, both right and not so right. You will also have a fair few tools you can choose from.

CI/CD

The first area to look into is your container delivery system. This is known as your continuous integration and continuous delivery system. These will help deploy your workload into your various environments and give you the flexibility to do much more with your container images or workload deployment. Table 6-6 lists a few options available for CI/CD pipelines.

Table 6-6. *CI/CD options*

Tool Name	Description
Jenkins	Popular free open source tool that's easy enough to use and has loads of plugin options
TeamCity	Integration with Visual Studio, useful for Windows development and testing. Has both free and proprietary options
GitLab	Has the ability to build and run tasks directly from your GitLab repositories
Travis CI	Can automatically detect commits in GitHub and run tests on a hosted Travis CI platform
Tekton	Another open source CI/CD tool that supports deployments across different cloud or on-premise platforms

Jenkins Example

Jenkins is one of the more popular pipelining tools to use today and is free to use for testing. To see what Jenkins pipeline code looks like, the following is a basic example using pseudo code:

```
node {
    def app

    stage('Clone repository') {
        /* Basic comment about cloning code*/
        checkout scm
    }

    stage('Build image') {
        /* Build your container image */
        app = docker.build("jenkinsproject/helloworld")
    }

    stage('Test image') {
        /* Run your unit testing of some type */
        app.inside {
            sh 'echo "Tests passed"'
        }
    }

    stage('Push image') {
        /* With a verified image, push your image to a registry */
        docker.withRegistry('https://someregistry.com',
        'registry-credentials') {
            app.push("${env.BUILD_NUMBER}")
            app.push("latest")
        }
    }
}
```

From this Jenkins example, you can see that stages are used in the pipeline; you can add as many as you like for different tasks. You may want to add a stage for security image scanning as an example. Ideally, you want to build in as much automation and testing as possible.

Challenge   As a learning challenge, deploy a Jenkins container on your sandbox environment or laptop. See if you can write your own custom Jenkins file to build a new container image that is triggered from your source code being updated in git.

Dedicated Image Builders

Make use of non-Docker components to build container images. Tools like Buildah (`https://buildah.io/`) and Kaniko (`https://github.com/GoogleContainerTools/kaniko`) are more secure as they run each command in the Dockerfile in userspace. Both Buildah and Kaniko do not require the Docker daemon to be running to build images.

Image Registry

As you develop your applications and container content, you will need a place to store these images. It is ok if you want to test and build when you need to, but as a good practice, it is recommended to start storing your container images as you start building your application portfolio. This practice is highly recommended if you are going to be deploying anything into a live environment.

Previously in this chapter, we discussed how to build a podman image registry; to extend on that, look at providing storage to ensure your containers are not ephemeral. Podman, for instance, has the ability to create volumes; those volumes can be mounted in your container when you create them.

Using orchestration platforms like OpenShift or Kubernetes can provide image registries but are often ephemeral by default. Ensure you have storage volumes mounted so you do not lose any of your images.

Development Editor Plugins

Using your development editor of choice, find and install plugins that help with container development debugging. Plugins that can assist with Dockerfile or Jenkinsfile creation will definitely help as you are starting out.

Tip   VSCode is a great option if you need something that's free and easy to use. Overall, for me it's a winner, but test it for yourself.

Linting Tools

Before pushing or committing any type of code, be it YAML or Dockerfiles, make use of linting tools. For Dockerfiles, there is a nice online linting tool you can copy and paste your Dockerfile content to be checked.

```
www.fromlatest.io/#/
```

DevSecOps

A keyword in today's world of platform management is DevOps. DevOps is a vital set of practices and tools that bridge the gap between developers and operational teams. DevSecOps is an addition to this concept, where everyone is responsible for security.

DevSecOps Tooling

DevSecOps empowers both developers and operational teams to understand security requirements and build security into their tooling.

Pipelines

In a standard situation where there are no DevOps or DevSecOps practices used, security teams are required to scan and report issues every time a new system or platform is built. Security teams are responsible for the organization's security and the ones who would have to answer the difficult questions if a breach is ever experienced. For this reason, they are meticulous in their scanning and ensuring no vulnerabilities are exposed in live environments. This process can involve additional security tools and can take time to be completed. This can also be a frustrating job if new platforms or systems are released constantly.

By following DevSecOps practices, security considerations can be built into pipeline or image building tools. With this process, developers and operational teams take responsibility for security, thus greatly reducing back and forth with security teams.

Security Gates

With security built into pipeline tools like Jenkins, security gates can be built where if an image fails a security scan for whatever reason, the build process can be stopped, allowing remediation to occur before being released into a live environment.

GitOps

Another keyword in today's estate management and container platform management is GitOps.

"GitOps is an operational framework that takes DevOps best practices used for application development such as version control, collaboration, compliance, and CI/CD tooling, and applies them to infrastructure automation."

```
https://about.gitlab.com/topics/gitops/
```

GitOps Toolbox

Some useful tools that can help you along your GitOps learning are as follows. There are many other tools and variations you can use, but as this subject can be one for a book on its own, I have mentioned only a few.

Git

The first step to using GitOps is to start using Git. This can be GitLab, Bitbucket, or GitHub, any Git platform that allows the ability for CI/CD pipelines to detect merge requests.

Infrastructure As Code

Technically not a tool, however, everything you write to automate or configure your platform should be in the form of code. That could be YAML for your OpenShift or Kubernetes configurations or Ansible to build a new system. Everything should be built or configured from code; no manual configuration should be used anywhere.

Pipeline Tools

Choose your pipeline tool and configure it to detect merge or pull requests in your git environment. Every time a new change is made, the pipeline should be kicked off to build or deploy new application versions or build new systems.

ArgoCD

Another GitOps tool being used more and more is ArgoCD. ArgoCD helps with GitOps workflows and can be used as a stand-alone tool or as a part of your CI/CD pipeline.

ArgoCD along with Git acts as a "source of truth" when configuring OpenShift or other Kubernetes variants. It's useful to maintain the state of your container orchestration platforms. It's very similar to how estate management tools like SaltStack maintain the state of systems within the estate it manages.

ArgoCD works with Git by paying attention to any configuration file changes through the means of pull or merge requests. When a change is merged in Git, ArgoCD pulls the new configuration and configures the platform the configuration is meant for (Figure 6-6).

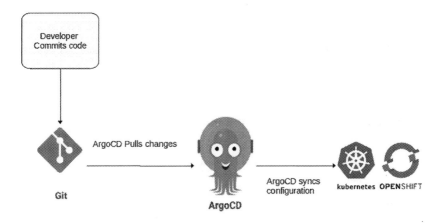

Figure 6-6.

Figure 6-6 shows the basic flow an ArgoCD configuration should take.

Container Orchestration

A few containers can quickly spiral into hundreds if not thousands in environments where applications are being deployed on a regular basis. To manage this kind of growth, the need for container orchestration becomes more important. Tools like Kubernetes, Docker Swarm, and OpenShift provide the ability for administrators to manage large estates of container workloads and ensure their availability. Each tool has its own advantages and disadvantages and could be discussed in such length it would take many more chapters to cover; however, as we are not focusing too much on container orchestration at the moment, let's just touch on the basics for now.

What Does It Do?

Container orchestration is the layer that must exist above containers before they are used by end users. A good container orchestration tool should have the following properties:

- Scalable
- Flexible
- Secure
- Automated
- Easy to use

These properties ensure that container workload can be managed effectively and securely, has the ability to plug in to CI/CD systems, and has content updated dynamically.

Why Not Use Podman?

The difference between using something like Podman to host an array of pods and Kubernetes as an example is Podman does not give you the ability to monitor performance and adjust the quantity of pods to handle additional load automatically.

Podman does not have the flexibility to create isolated networks between different nodes for specific workload.

All these higher-level configuration and automation services that are provided by orchestration layers like Kubernetes or OpenShift are meant for large estate deployments. Podman has the ability to host a multitude of pods with many containers inside but lacks the ability to manage these pods at scale. Adding more nodes and connecting pod networks would prove more complicated and would defeat the purpose of a container orchestration layer being easy to use.

Podman is useful for local or small deployments but not meant for anything at scale. You can develop your own wrapping tools to manage Podman, but you would just be reinventing the wheel. The best thing to do would be to invest your time using Kubernetes or another enterprise product like OpenShift if you can get your hands on it. Failing that, you can also use the community product called OKD.

Orchestration Options

Kubernetes

Kubernetes, or K8s, is an open source project that was originally developed by Google and based on their original "Borg" system (cluster manager system).

Red Hat was one of the first contributors to Kubernetes before it was officially launched.

In 2015, Google donated the Kubernetes project to the CNCF (Cloud Native Computing Foundation).

Kubernetes Forks

As Kubernetes is open sourced, there are many downstream variations of Kubernetes today like Red Hat's OpenShift, VMware's version of Kubernetes, and many cloud platforms like AWS and Azure providing their own managed services.

These cloud managed services allow end users to deploy their container workloads without the need to build their own orchestration platform or manage any of the systems associated with it. Users sign up for an account, get allocated resources, and deploy workloads.

Where OpenShift and Kubernetes can be deployed in the cloud and on-premise, they need to be installed, configured, and managed going forward. This is useful if you need to deploy very large estates and are happy to do all the administration yourself.

Master Components

Kubernetes has a few fundamental cluster components that enable it to provide the orchestration for pods and the containers within.

The Control Plane

The control plane consists of the following:

- The ETCD key value database that stores all the cluster configuration

- The API server that provides the Kubernetes API via JSON over http

- The scheduler which is responsible for scheduling workload on nodes

- The controller manager used to manage different Kubernetes controllers

The control plane is provided by a cluster of master nodes; these nodes replicate configuration between them to ensure the control continues to provide the cluster functionality.

Nodes

Nodes are the workers of the Kubernetes clusters. They are responsible for hosting the container workload users deploy. Nodes consist of a few subcomponents:

- Kubelet ensures the state of the node and the health of containers running on it.

- Kube-proxy is responsible for routing traffic to your containers.

- Container runtime.

Namespaces

Namespaces are designed to provide a way to segregate one Kubernetes cluster so multiple users could deploy workloads without being able to communicate with each other.

Daemonsets

Normally, the scheduler is responsible for placing pods on nodes where resources are available to ensure that not only one node gets overloaded. Daemonsets, however, are used when you need to force a pod to run on each node. This is often the case with logging containers.

Worker Node Components

Workload objects are what is deployed and used on worker nodes. The following are used on most if not all worker nodes.

Pods

Containers are run within pods; these pods are what are spawned on worker nodes. Typically, one container is run within one pod, but this is not a hard and fast rule.

Services

Services are what binds multiple pods of the same application together. When multiple pods are spawned on different worker nodes, you need to balance traffic between them. A service is the layer that provides that "service."

Volumes

By default, all containers are ephemeral, which means they have no way to store their data after a pod restart or recreation. By mounting volumes or persistent volumes to pods, you are to recover any data from previously destroyed or restarted pods.

Configmaps

Within containers, you sometimes need to configure configuration files. A web server, for instance, may need to be configured with details about the website it is hosting. Configmaps give you the ability to abstract the configuration from the container image to the orchestration platform. When a pod is deployed with a configmap, the configuration is then applied during the deployment phase, similar to how Dockerfiles can be used to configure the container image.

OpenShift

Before OpenShift was OpenShift, it was a PaaS product by a company called Makara. Red Hat acquired Makara in 2010 for the PaaS platform which was proprietary at the time based on Linux container technology.

Early OpenShift

Prior to OpenShift 3.0, the Red Hat PaaS platform was proprietary and custom developed. It took two years after the acquisition for Red Hat to release the first open sourced version and then three years after that to move away from the custom platform to a more "mature" Kubernetes at the time.

OpenShift 3.0 was the first release where Red Hat used Docker for the container runtime and Kubernetes for the orchestration layer.

OpenShift 3.11 was the last minor release of OpenShift 3 and the last version where Docker was used as the container runtime.

Current OpenShift

Red Hat currently has OpenShift 4.9 generally available for public use. The detachment of the "hardcoded" Docker has allowed OpenShift 4.x to move to a container runtime interface approach where any low-level container runtime can be used.

OpenShift has matured to become the leading container orchestration platform for the enterprise and thus has become the number one container orchestration product for many organizations. Red Hat's continued investment continues to grow OpenShift new functionality and acquisitions.

Advanced Cluster Security (StackRox), Advanced Cluster Management, monitoring, logging, and many other enterprise-grade features make OpenShift the go-to product for any serious hybrid cloud organization.

OpenShift Components

As OpenShift is based on Kubernetes, most of the components are very similar and named in a very similar manner. There are of course some variations, like namespaces in Kubernetes are referred to as projects in

OpenShift. The kube command with Kubernetes is the "oc" command with OpenShift, but most importantly the following are some of the major differences.

Product

OpenShift is a product, not a project like Kubernetes. Kubernetes is a community project that anyone can contribute to. These changes do make their way into OpenShift if Red Hat deems them useful.

Enterprise

The enterprise vs. community argument again, OpenShift is an enterprise product where Kubernetes is a community project. There are paid enterprise support options that companies like Google provide but are still based on the community project.

Security

OpenShift has been built with security in mind, opening the adoption for more security conscious organizations. The recent acquisition of StackRox has only strengthened this argument even more.

Web Console

OpenShift has a web console by default. Kubernetes requires you to deploy it separately and have the cluster kube-proxy direct traffic to the console.

Many More

Without listing all the differences, there are other features like image management and enterprise storage solutions that Red Hat OpenShift provides over Kubernetes. If you are interested, you should do as recommended with most products in this book. Build a proof of concept and compare the differences for yourself.

Summary

In this chapter, you were introduced to the following:

- An overview of what containers are, their runtimes, how to build a container, and how containers are customized

- Some practical uses of containers and how to create a local container registry

- What cloud native means and the various good and bad practices of using containers

- Different container tooling along with DevSecOps and GitOps practices

- Container orchestration and what options are available for you to use

PART III

Day Two Practices and Keeping the Lights On

During Part 2, we discussed how you can improve what you are doing by exploring what tooling you could or should be using. These initial chapters were written in such a way to open your mind to the possibility of doing more with less. We spoke about management tools, automation, and containerization.

The goal of this part is to look at how you can continue to keep the lights on, what tools you should consider using, and how you should be keeping your environment as secure as possible while being flexible enough to not restrict innovation.

CHAPTER 7

Monitoring

What are some of the most important features any new Linux system must have before it can be accepted into your organization's production or live estate? The common answers given are monitoring, logging, and security. For good reason too, any system that is not being monitored, logged, or secure is just a recipe for disaster and in almost every single case will be rejected by any serious operations team.

This chapter will take a deeper look at one of the first things a Linux system should have: monitoring. We will discuss tools that have been used in the past and what tools are available out of the box with most Linux distros. We will then look at some of the newer tools and trends that have been used within the last five years.

Finally, we will discuss what developers and applications require from a monitoring point of view, how applications can be better monitored, and how to initiate discussions with developers on how to develop applications to support this. This chapter will not give you all the answers to all the different monitoring use cases. It will give you ideas on what you could be doing and what tooling could help with some of your current monitoring questions. It may even create a few questions you did not realize you needed to ask.

© Kenneth Hitchcock 2022
K. Hitchcock, *Linux System Administration for the 2020s*,
https://doi.org/10.1007/978-1-4842-7984-7_7

Linux Monitoring Tools

Almost as long as Linux has been around, there have been tools to monitor what is happening on the system. These tools could be as basic as the "top" command or as complex as using systemtap to understand what the kernel is doing when a new device is added to your system.

Once you know the basics on how to use a Linux system, the next logical step should always be to know how to confirm your system is healthy and how to ensure it stays that way. For this, there are numerous different tools that can show your system state.

Process Monitoring

Default Process Commands, ps and top

By default, on most if not all Linux distros, you will find both the "top" and "ps" commands. They not only show you all the processes running on your system but also give you the process ID number that can be used to kill a defunct or hung process.

If you are not sure a particular process is running, for instance, the apache web service, you can run a command similar to the following:

```
# ps -ef | grep httpd
```

The "top" or the alternative commands could also be used, but you may struggle to search through the list for your process. Using "ps" and "grep" will give you a quicker and cleaner output.

Note   During Chapter 2, we looked at "top" and a few other tools that could be used to find running processes on your system. We also discussed how to kill processes and how to identify zombie processes.

Pstree

A quick and nice tool to see all the processes and the parents of each process is the "pstree" command. The following is a basic output of pstree with a reduced output:

```
# pstree
systemd─┬─ModemManager────3*[{ModemManager}]
        ├─NetworkManager────2*[{NetworkManager}]
        ├─abrt-dbus────2*[{abrt-dbus}]
        ├─3*[abrt-dump-journ]
        ├─abrtd────2*[{abrtd}]
        ... [reduced for length]
        ├─thermald────{thermald}
        ├─udisksd────4*[{udisksd}]
        ├─upowerd────2*[{upowerd}]
        ├─uresourced────2*[{uresourced}]
        └─wpa_supplicant
```

Resource-Hungry Processes

The "ps" command is useful for another reason. I'm sure you have experienced a process that has been CPU or memory intensive. Finding that offending process can sometimes be a bit tricky if you are trying to figure out how processes are consuming resources from the "top" or similar commands. The following are two "ps" commands you can use to find the top five CPU- and memory-intensive processes.

Memory-Intensive Processes

```
# ps -auxf | sort -nr -k 4 | head -5
```

CPU-Intensive Processes

```
# ps -auxf | sort -nr -k 3 | head -5
```

Tip   Look at the ps --help and ps man pages for more options to use with ps.

Disk and IO

There could be a situation where you have slow disk performance or disks filling up. Some useful tools that can be used for disk and IO monitoring that are still used today are tools like "iostat," "iotop," "du," and "df."

iostat and iotop

"iostat" and "iotop" are basic tools that give you information about your input-output systems:

```
# iostat
Linux 5.13.4-200.fc34.x86_64 (localhost.
localdomain)        22/11/21      _x86_64_        (4 CPU)

avg-cpu:  %user   %nice %system %iowait  %steal   %idle
          28.17    0.06   12.21    0.11    0.00   59.46

Device              tps    kB_read/s    kB_wrtn/s    kB_dscd/s
    kB_read     kB_wrtn     kB_dscd
dm-0               1.16         1.79        59.42        24.16
    16712024  554638596   225476964
nvme0n1            1.15         1.79        59.43        24.24
    16724756  554741532   226295700
zram0              0.20         0.16         0.64         0.00
     1482776    6013392           0
```

```
# iotop
Total DISK READ:         0.00 B/s | Total DISK WRITE:    108.61 K/s
Current DISK READ:       0.00 B/s | Current DISK WRITE:    3.19 K/s
    TID  PRIO  USER      DISK READ  DISK WRITE  SWAPIN    IO>
COMMAND
 733973 be/4 ken          0.00 B/s  57.50 K/s  0.00 %  0.00 %
chrome --type=utility --utility-sub-type=network.mojom.
NetworkService --field-trial-han~be2ad25, --shared-files=v8_
context_snapshot_data:100 --enable-crashpad [ThreadPoolForeg]
 729143 be/4 root         0.00 B/s  51.11 K/s  0.00 %  0.00 %
[kworker/u8:6-btrfs-endio-write]
      1 be/4 root         0.00 B/s   0.00 B/s  0.00 %  0.00 %
      systemd rhgb --system --deserialize 51
      2 be/4 root         0.00 B/s   0.00 B/s  0.00 %  0.00 %
      [kthreadd]
      3 be/0 root         0.00 B/s   0.00 B/s  0.00 %  0.00 %
      [rcu_gp]
      4 be/0 root         0.00 B/s   0.00 B/s  0.00 %  0.00 %
      [rcu_par_gp]
```

du and df

These are used to show disk usage and where disks are mounted:

```
# df -h
Filesystem      Size  Used  Avail  Use%  Mounted on
devtmpfs        12G    0     12G    0%   /dev
tmpfs           12G   181M   12G    2%   /dev/shm
tmpfs          4.7G   2.0M  4.7G    1%   /run
/dev/dm-0      238G    93G  144G   40%   /
tmpfs           12G    61M   12G    1%   /tmp
/dev/dm-0      238G    93G  144G   40%   /home
```

```
/dev/nvme0n1p1  976M  272M  638M  30% /boot
tmpfs           2.4G  216K  2.4G   1% /run/user/1000

# du -h /etc
0        /etc/.java/.systemPrefs
8.0K     /etc/.java/deployment
8.0K     /etc/.java
0        /etc/NetworkManager/conf.d
0        /etc/NetworkManager/dispatcher.d/no-wait.d
0        /etc/NetworkManager/dispatcher.d/pre-down.d
0        /etc/NetworkManager/dispatcher.d/pre-up.d
0        /etc/NetworkManager/dispatcher.d
0        /etc/NetworkManager/dnsmasq-shared.d
0        /etc/NetworkManager/dnsmasq.d
28K      /etc/NetworkManager/system-connections
32K      /etc/NetworkManager
... [reduced for length]
80K      /etc/gimp/2.0
80K      /etc/gimp
28K     /etc/pcp/derived
28K     /etc/pcp
37M     /etc/
```

CPU

CPU statistics on your system can be checked using a number of tools both shipped with your distro and tools that you can install quite easily. The following are two of the more common tools used.

Top

Most Linux sysadmins will use the top command and press the "1" key.
This will give a similar output to the following:

```
top - 23:56:10 up 108 days,  1:38,  1 user,  load average:
1.31, 1.73, 1.54
Tasks: 373 total,   2 running, 370 sleeping,   0 stopped,
1 zombie
%Cpu0  : 10.0 us,  2.3 sy,  0.0 ni, 87.0 id,  0.0 wa,  0.3 hi,
0.3 si,  0.0 st
%Cpu1  :  6.6 us,  7.9 sy,  0.0 ni, 83.8 id,  0.0 wa,  1.0 hi,
0.7 si,  0.0 st
%Cpu2  : 10.7 us,  3.3 sy,  0.0 ni, 85.3 id,  0.0 wa,  0.3 hi,
0.3 si,  0.0 st
%Cpu3  : 10.3 us,  3.6 sy,  0.0 ni, 83.4 id,  0.3 wa,  2.0 hi,
0.3 si,  0.0 st
MiB Mem :  23679.7 total,   3091.2 free,  13131.6 used,
7456.8 buff/cache
MiB Swap:   8192.0 total,   6207.6 free,   1984.4 used.
8940.7 avail Mem

    PID USER      PR  NI    VIRT    RES    SHR S  %CPU  %MEM
    TIME+ COMMAND
   2021 ken       20   0 1448452 123008  73736 S  18.2   0.5
   252:05.89 Xorg
 728039 ken       20   0  749048  52472  36696 S   6.9   0.2
 6:54.61 gnome-system-mo
```

From the preceding output, you can see that I have four cores in my
laptop. The load average can be seen to be around 1.33, which means that
around 1.33 of my four CPUs are currently being used to run processes.

mpstat

Another useful command for CPU statistics is the mpstat command. The "mpstat" command displays activities for each available CPU.

To see all the stats per CPU, you can run the following command:

```
# mpstat -P ALL
```

Memory

A few ways to check system memory include looking at the /proc/meminfo file or running commands like "free" or "top." The following are a few things you can do on your system to understand more about its memory.

Free

Basic utility that gives all the information required about your system's memory:

```
# free -h
          total     used     free    shared   buff/cache   available
Mem:       23Gi     12Gi    3.2Gi    1.2Gi         7.2Gi        8.8Gi
Swap:     8.0Gi    1.9Gi    6.1Gi
```

Page Size

If you need to find out your system's page size, you can use the following commands:

```
# getconf PAGESIZE
```

Huge Page Size

When doing application server tuning, you may be asked to enable or check if HugePage sizing has been enabled. You can check this in the /proc/meminfo file:

```
# cat /proc/meminfo |grep Hugepage
Hugepagesize:        2048 kB
```

pmap

Another useful tool is the "pmap" utility. "pmap" reports a memory map of a process. "pmap" can be quite useful to find causes of memory bottlenecks.

Virtual Memory

It does occasionally happen that you need to investigate issues around virtual memory or slabinfo. The "vmstat" tool is useful for this kind of investigation.

vmstat

The vmstat tool can be run to give you different information about your system.

Running a basic vmstat command as follows:

```
# vmstat
```

will give you the following output, which is explained in Table 7-1:

```
procs -----------memory---------- ---swap-- -----io----
-system-- ------cpu-----
 r  b  swpd    free    buff  cache   si  so  bi   bo   in  cs
us sy id wa st
 0  0  2032024  2086144  1056  8923084   2   8  21  701  40  50
28 12 59  0  0
```

Table 7-1. *vmstat output explained*

vmstat Column	Description
r	The number of processes waiting for runtime
b	The number of processes in uninterruptible sleep
swpd	Virtual memory used
free	Idle memory
buff	Memory used as buffers
cache	Memory used as cache
si	Memory swapped in from disk
so	Memory swapped to disk
bi	Blocks received from a block device
bo	Blocks sent to a block device
in	Interrupts per second
cs	Number of context switches per second
us	Percentage of time running non-kernel code
sy	Percentage of time running kernel code
id	Percentage of time spent idle
wa	Percentage of time spent waiting for IO

Network

Tools to monitor network configuration or traffic are really useful when you need to troubleshoot issues or confirm a port is listening for traffic. The following are a few tools I have used in the past.

Netstat

One of the first tools I tend to use when I need to check if a port is listening for traffic is the "netstat" command.

The "netstat" command will show you network connections, interface statistics, and more. The most common commands I use to check what ports are listening are as follows:

```
# nestat -nap | grep LIST
# netstat -planet
```

Note   Netstat is still part of the net-tools package but at some point will be removed as netstat is now obsolete; it is preferred to use the ss command instead.

---

ss

To get some quick information about socket statistics, you can use the "ss" command.

To view all TCP and UDP sockets on a Linux system with ss, you can use the following command:

```
# ss -t -a
```

iptraf-ng

If you prefer to use initiative tools to view network statistics, you can use the "iptraf" command. "iptraf" is useful to monitor various network statistics including TCP info, UDP counts, interface load info, IP checksum errors, and loads of other useful information (Figure 7-1).

```
# iptraf-ng
```

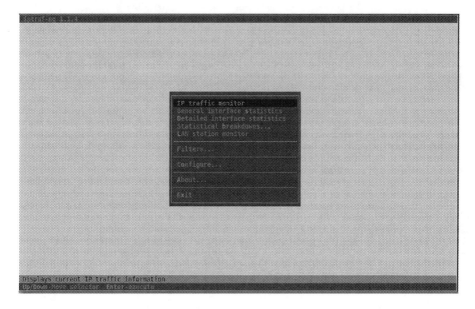

Figure 7-1.

Figure 7-1 is what you are presented with when you open iptraf-ng.

This tool has helped me on a few occasions where I needed to monitor the traffic out of a particular interface. It is not installed by default but definitely worth using if you are not already.

From the main screen, you can select to monitor IP traffic; from there, you select the interface you want to monitor, then watch the connectivity over that interface.

Tcpdump

Most if not all network engineers will use wireshark to monitor traffic on their network. The "tcpdump" command allows the Linux sysadmin to dump traffic on a particular network interface, all interfaces, or for a particular service like DHCP or DNS.

If you wanted to monitor all traffic on interface eth0 for anything sending traffic to port 80, in the case of a web server, you could run a similar command:

```
# tcpdump -n -i eth0 -s 0 -w tcpdumpoutput.txt src or
dst port 80
```

The output file from the preceding command can then be opened using the wireshark tool (Figure 7-2).

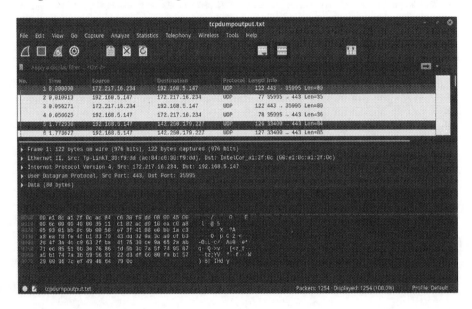

Figure 7-2.

Note   A useful way to look for anything that could be transmitting on your network in clear text.

NetHogs

If you were experiencing high bursts of network load on a Linux system and wanted to know who could be responsible, you can try the "nethogs" tool to see which PID is causing a bandwidth situation (Figure 7-3).

```
# nethogs
```

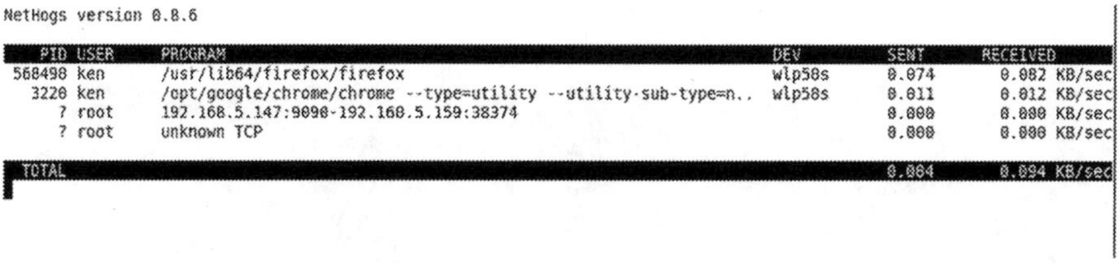

```
NetHogs version 0.8.6

   PID USER    PROGRAM                                                    DEV     SENT     RECEIVED
568498 ken     /usr/lib64/firefox/firefox                                wlp58s  0.074    0.082 KB/sec
  3220 ken     /opt/google/chrome/chrome --type=utility --utility-sub-type=n..  wlp58s  0.011    0.012 KB/sec
     ? root    192.168.5.147:9090-192.168.5.159:38374                             0.000    0.000 KB/sec
     ? root    unknown TCP                                                        0.000    0.000 KB/sec

 TOTAL                                                                            0.004    0.094 KB/sec
```

Figure 7-3.

    NetHogs groups bandwidth by process name such as Firefox and chrome as you can see in Figure 7-3.

iftop

This is a simple command very similar to "top" but for interface information (Figure 7-4).

```
# iftop
```

```
                12.5Kb              25.0Kb          37.5Kb            50.0Kb          62.5Kb
         └─────────────┴───────────────┴──────────────┴───────────┴──────────────┴
localhost.localdomain            => 7.91.93.34.bc.googleusercontent.com       0b    2.29Kb   1.64Kb
                                 <=                                            0b    8.46Kb   6.04Kb
localhost.localdomain            => dns.google                              620b    1.64Kb   1.17Kb
                                 <=                                          620b    1.89Kb   1.35Kb
localhost.localdomain            => 137.39.190.35.bc.googleusercontent.com    0b     761b     543b
                                 <=                                            0b     558b     399b
localhost.localdomain            => lhr48s28-in-f10.1e100.net                 0b     694b     495b
                                 <=                                            0b     499b     357b
224.0.0.251                      => 192.168.5.102                             0b      0b       0b
                                 <=                                            0b    1.12kb    822b
localhost.localdomain            => lhr48s27-in-f10.1e100.net                 0b     396b     283b
                                 <=                                            0b     222b     158b
255.255.255.255                  => 192.168.5.185                             0b      0b       0b
                                 <=                                          812b     407b     464b
localhost.localdomain            => 192.168.5.102                             0b     221b     158b
                                 <=                                            0b     157b     112b
255.255.255.255                  => 192.168.5.117                             0b      0b       0b
                                 <=                                            0b     346b     247b
224.0.0.251                      => 192.168.5.121                             0b      0b       0b
                                 <=                                            0b     326b     233b
224.0.0.251                      => 192.168.5.122                             0b      0b       0b
                                 <=                                            0b     326b     233b
255.255.255.255                  => 192.168.5.187                             0b      0b       0b
                                 <=                                          812b     325b     348b
255.255.255.255                  => 192.168.5.154                             0b      0b       0b
                                 <=                                            0b     320b     229b
255.255.255.255                  => 192.168.5.116                             0b      0b       0b
                                 <=                                            0b     160b     114b
192.168.5.255                    => 192.168.5.10                              0b      0b       0b
                                 <=                                            0b     157b     112b
─────────────────────────────────────────────────────────────────────────────────────────────
TX:          cum:    8.00KB   peak:   18.7Kb                      rates:    876b    6.40Kb   4.57Kb
RX:                 19.8KB            38.6Kb                                2.35Kb  15.6Kb   11.3Kb
TOTAL:              27.8KB            47.3Kb                                3.20Kb  22.0Kb   15.9Kb
```

Figure 7-4.

From Figure 7-4, you can see the layout of iftop is similar to the regular top output, except more focused on network data.

Graphical Tools

Gnome System Monitor

Linux desktops like Gnome are not without their own monitoring tools you can use. Those familiar with Windows will know about "task manager," a simple tool that gives you a basic rundown of what processes are running and the current performance of your system. The Gnome system monitor is not massively different. The first tab gives you a process list, the second tab lists your CPU and memory resources being used, and the last tab gives you a breakdown of your mounted filesystems (Figure 7-5).

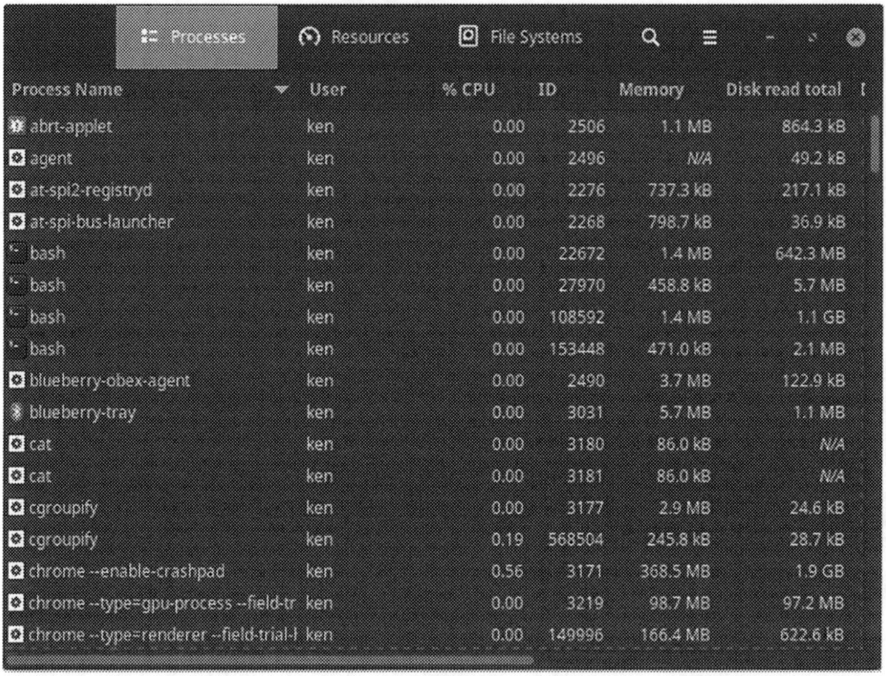

Figure 7-5.

From Figure 7-5, you can see all processes currently running on your Linux system.

Ksysguard

If the Gnome tool does not work for you, you can also use the KDE tool called ksysguard. The difference between the Gnome system monitor and the KDE ksysguard tool is that ksysguard has the ability to monitor remote systems. New tabs can be created, and different resources from remote systems can be monitored. Useful for a quick and simple monitoring tool with little to no real effort to configure (Figure 7-6).

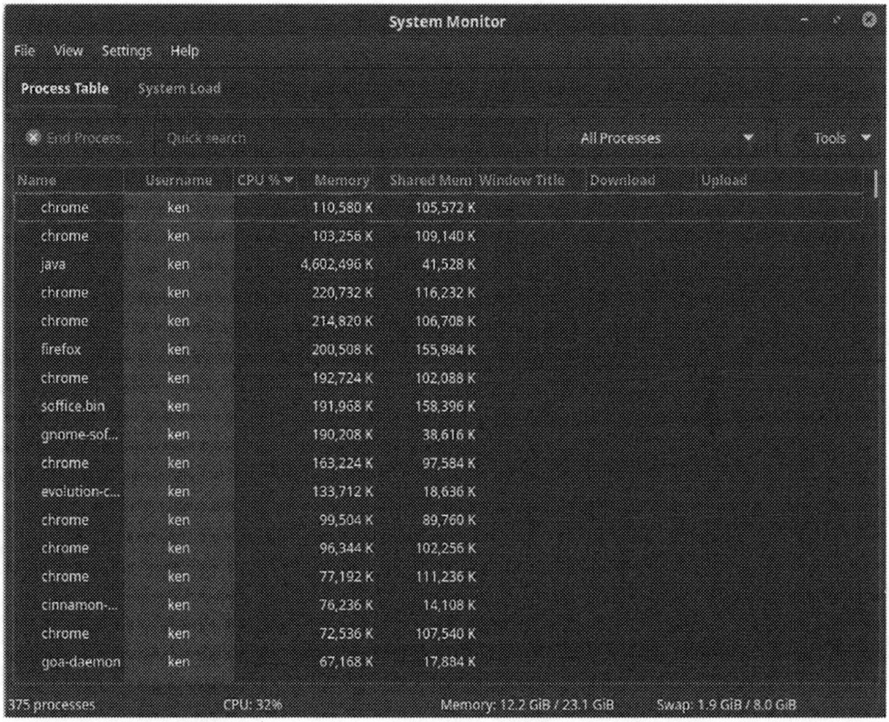

Figure 7-6.

Similar to the Gnome system monitor, you can also view all the processes running on your system, as demonstrated in Figure 7-6.

Historical Monitoring Data

So far, we have looked at some useful monitoring tools that can be used on a Linux distro but all with one issue (except maybe tcpdump). None of the tools keep historical data. The statistics shown are real-time data from your system at the current time. A simple example of wanting to see what CPU load was like from a previous day. Top and other such commands would not be of any use.

This is why the previous tools mentioned are for current system activity and real-time system checking. Trying to use them for root cause analysis after an issue has occurred will leave you with limited options.

Sar

A useful tool to query history system metrics is "sar." The "sar" utility is installed with the sysstat package. Along with "sar," the sysstat package has a few other utilities like iostat, mpstat, and nfsiostat, to name a few.

The "sar" utility stores system statistics and metrics within local system files that can be queried later for system statistics. The sar files can be found at the following location:

/var/log/sa/

Common sar parameters are explained in Table 7-2.

Table 7-2. sar options

Switch	Description
d	Block device statistics
r	Memory utilization
u	CPU utilization
F	Filesystem statistics

Performance Co-Pilot

A utility that is a bit better to use in my opinion over "sar" is the tools installed with the pcp package. The pcp package installs a few useful tools for metric querying and metric collection. Table 7-3 lists the tools installed with the pcp package.

Table 7-3. *pcp tools*

Name	Description
pmstat	Live information about your system, CPU, memory, etc.
pminfo	Lists the metrics that can be queried
pmval	Views the metric data
pmlogger	Stores the metric data into files that can be queried later by pmval

vnstat

Not to forget network metrics, the vnstat tool is another useful tool to keep historical network information. vnstat keeps a log of hourly, daily, and monthly network traffic for the selected interface or interfaces.

Central Monitoring

With a good understanding now of local monitoring and metric collection tools, we can now move on to central monitoring tools available in the open source world. These are the tools that can be used to monitor your entire estate from a single location with historical data being kept for potential root cause analysis later down the line.

Nagios

The first tool that many people may know and have come to use at some point is Nagios. Nagios is another one of those open source names that is recursive. Nagios means "Nagios ain't going to insist on sainthood."

Versions

Nagios has both a community and a paid-for product that can be installed on most Linux distros. CentOS and RHEL, however, are the supported platforms at this stage for the Enterprise Nagios XI product. Nagios Core, however, can be installed on quite a few different Linux distros. It's always best to discuss these options with the vendor if you ever decide to use the paid-for product.

Core

The community supported edition of Nagios is the Core release which gives you the basic monitoring capabilities of Nagios but requires you to use community forums for help and support.

Nagios XI

The enterprise or paid-for solution of Nagios comes with the standard core components plus more. This also includes all the support for the product via phone and email.

Agent Based

Nagios consists of a server and agent-based deployment with a few options around agents that can be used.

NRPE

Nagios Remote Plugin Executor (NRPE) uses scripts that are hosted on the client systems. NRPE can monitor resources like disk usage, system load, or total number of logged in users. Nagios periodically polls the agent on the remote systems using the check_nrpe plugin.

NRPE can also communicate with Windows agent add-ons, allowing Nagios to execute scripts and check metrics on remote Windows machines.

Note   NRPE has since been deprecated and is here only for information.

NRDP

NRDP or Nagios Remote Data Processor is another Nagios agent you can use. NRDP comes with a flexible data transport mechanism and processor allowing NRDP to be easily extended and customized. NRDP uses standard ports and protocols (HTTP and XML) and can be used in place of NSCA (Nagios Service Check Acceptor).

NSClient++

A Windows agent for Nagios, NSClient++ listens on TCP ports through to 12489. The Nagios plugin that is used to collect information from this add-on is called check_nt.

NSClient++ is similar to NRPE, as it allows Nagios to monitor memory usage, CPU load, disk usage, etc.

NCPA

The final agent that can be used is the NCPA agent. The NCPA or Nagios Cross Platform Agent is an open source project maintained by Nagios Enterprises.

NCPA can be installed on Windows and Linux. Unlike other agents, NCPA makes use of the API to gather information and metrics for Nagios. Active checks are done through the API of the "NCPA Listener" service, while passive checks are sent via the "NCPA Passive" service.

Nagios Forks

There are a number of forks from Nagios that can also be used. Some of the forks of Nagios are as follows:

- Icinga

- Naemon

- Shinken

All will share a similarity with Nagios but over time have evolved into their own solutions. Icinga, for instance, has been developing its own features for well over a decade now.

Installation

The installation for Nagios can be done in a few ways and is well documented on the Nagios documentation site:

- Follow the official documentation and run steps one by one.

- Build a virtual machine and run automation scripts.

- Pull a Nagios container image and run a container.

The recommended approach would be to use automation tooling like Ansible to deploy Nagios within a dedicated system, but for quick testing and playing, use a container.

Prometheus

Prometheus is an open source alerting and event monitoring system that stores data in a time series database. Prometheus is a central location for metric data to be stored and is usually paired with other software to provide an overall monitoring solution.

Exporters

Exporters are what gets data to Prometheus's time series database. Multiple exporters can be used on client or server systems. There are dedicated exporters for different purposes; in the case of getting node information, there is a dedicated node_exporter that will export local system metrics like CPU or memory utilization.

Alert Tool

Any monitoring platform worth its weight in salt must have a way to tell Linux sysadmins when there is a problem. This is typically your alerting tool. A useful open source tool is Alertmanager, which can be used to trigger alerts based on Prometheus metrics.

Dashboarding

Even though Prometheus does have a web UI that can be used to query metrics, it makes more sense to send metrics to a dashboarding tool. Grafana, for instance, is a good choice for this and is one of the more popular open source tools available today.

Query Language

PromQL is the query language used to create dashboards and alerts.

Installation

In the same way it is recommended to install Nagios, I would recommend to install Prometheus. The documentation is very clear and well thought through. The installation steps are simple enough if you want to do it manually, but I would still advise the automated method. The Internet is full of Ansible roles to do it for you, or if you prefer, there are also container images that can be used to deploy a container if you want the prebuilt option.

Kubernetes or OpenShift

Platforms like Kubernetes or OpenShift can also have Prometheus deployed on them, but they tend to be used for the platform itself. You would need to create a new namespace and deploy your own Prometheus and Grafana to use for external system monitoring.

Configuration

Once installed, Prometheus does not require much configuration to get started. A simple YAML file normally named prometheus.yaml can be used for all configurations. A basic configuration from the official Prometheus site is as follows:

```
global:
  scrape_interval:     15s
  evaluation_interval: 15s

rule_files:
  # - "first.rules"
  # - "second.rules"

scrape_configs:
  - job_name: prometheus
    static_configs:
      - targets: ['localhost:9090']
```

Global

The global section is for Prometheus global configuration. General configuration to tell Prometheus how often to scrape, for instance.

Rule_files

The rule_files section is for custom rules we want Prometheus to use. The example configuration in this case does not have any rule_files to use.

Scrape_configs

The scrape_configs section tells Prometheus what metrics to gather. In the configuration example, the localhost will be contacted on port 9090 and will search for metrics on the /metrics endpoint.

Starting Prometheus

Typically, monitoring platforms should be started from a service, and Prometheus can be configured to do so too. When starting Prometheus, you should have at least one parameter specified, and that is the name of the Prometheus configuration file you are using.

To start Prometheus manually, you can run the following command from the Prometheus installed directory:

```
# ./prometheus --config.file=prometheus.yml
```

Thanos

Prometheus monitoring is quite good on its own and can provide everything you might want from a simple monitoring platform, except maybe long historical data or high availability.

This is where Thanos can be utilized. Thanos has been designed to provide a highly available solution that can keep an unlimited metric retention from multiple Prometheus deployments.

Thanos is based on Prometheus and requires at least one Prometheus instance within the same network as itself. Thanos manages the metric collection and querying through a series of components.

Sidecar

A sidecar is the component that allows Thanos to connect to a Prometheus instance. It can then read data for querying or for uploading to cloud storage.

Store Gateway

This allows the querying of metric data inside a cloud object storage bucket.

Compactor

This compresses or compacts data and applies retention on the data stored in a cloud storage bucket.

Receiver

This is the component responsible for receiving data from Prometheus's remote-write function. The receiver can also expose metrics or upload it to cloud storage.

Ruler/Rule

This is used to evaluate recordings and alerting rules against data in Thanos.

Querier

This makes use of Prometheus's v1 API to pull and query data from underlying components.

Query Frontend

By using Prometheus's v1 API, the query frontend can evaluate PromQL queries against all instances at once.

Thanos Basic Layout

Figure 7-7 is a very basic illustration of how the various Thanos components speak to each other.

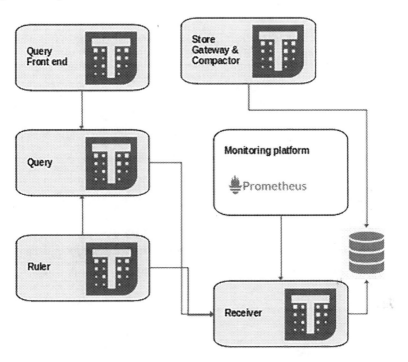

Figure 7-7.

Enterprise Monitoring

Monitoring for large organizations with different teams is normally a contentious subject, mostly because different teams all want to use a tool that suits them better. There are some excellent proprietary Windows tools, and then there are quite good open source Linux tools too that can be used. As this book is focused on open source technologies and the adoption of Linux, let's have a brief look at some open source enterprise monitoring tools that you could use.

Zabbix

A great enterprise-grade monitoring tool that can be used to monitor your estate is Zabbix. Zabbix pride themselves in the fact that they can monitor anything from server platforms through to network systems. Zabbix is a server- and agent-based system but can also monitor some facilities without the use of an agent.

Enterprise Support

Zabbix has a paid support facility that can be used for enterprise support, or you can support yourself through community forums.

Installation

The installation is relatively simple and is well documented on the Zabbix website. They have a really nice way of presenting the installation steps through a series of selection boxes based on your preferences.

Useful Features

There are a few really nice features that Zabbix can provide. Examples of these include the ability to monitor Java-based applications directly over JMX, the ability to monitor virtual machines with VMware tooling, and the ability to integrate with systems management tools like Puppet or Chef.

CheckMk

Another good enterprise monitoring tool is CheckMk. CheckMk is a scalable solution like Zabbix that can monitor a wide variety of systems from standard Linux platforms through to IoT devices.

Enterprise Support

CheckMk offers both a free version with unlimited monitoring where you support yourself and an enterprise paid-for solution with added features.

Installation

The major enterprise Linux distros are supported, and the CheckMk documentation has well-documented steps for whichever distro you are using.

Useful Features

CheckMk has been building their platform with the future in mind. They have built in the facilities to monitor Docker, Kubernetes, and Azure, to name a few.

The overall solution is scalable and will work well in large organizations with a distributed layout (multiple data centers). Automation has been one of the main development points to ensure that configuration and setup is as simple as possible.

OpenNMS

The first monitoring tool I ever installed was OpenNMS many years back when I first got into open source technologies. Researching for this book, I was quite impressed to see that not only was OpenNMS still a developed product, but it also looked pretty impressive.

Enterprise Support

Like most enterprise platforms, there are generally two options: a "free" version with community support and an enterprise paid version.

The OpenNMS versions are as follows:

- Horizon: The community-driven and supported version

- Meridian: The subscription-based service that provides the latest stable enterprise release

Installation

The installation of OpenNMS is not as simple as maybe some of the other tools available but in the same breath is not drastically difficult to install either. The official documentation is clear enough and does step you through everything you need to do. There is also a good community forum for questions if you get stuck.

Useful Features

One feature that really jumps out is that OpenNMS uses Grafana as a dashboarding tool, which, in my opinion, was an excellent move, largely due to the fact that more and more of today's users are developing their own dashboards.

OpenNMS metrics can also be collected with a wide variety of methods including JMX, WMI, HTML, XML, and more.

Dashboards

One aspect of monitoring that is almost as important as the metrics being collected is the ability to view metrics in a format that makes sense. This is where dashboarding tools are vital.

Over the years, I have come across a few monitoring tools that were and still are very good but just look awful in a browser. With some application monitoring tools, I also found the dashboards to be very difficult to configure. Sizing windows was a nightmare, and connecting external tools was always not possible.

It seems that I was not the only one to suffer with these tools, and some smart people have started developing dedicated dashboarding tools that can integrate with a variety of tools.

Dashboarding Tools

Table 7-4 lists a few dashboarding tools that can be used today.

Table 7-4. *Dashboarding tools*

Name	Description
Grafana	The most popular dashboarding tool available today. Originally released in 2013
Chronograf	A very good tool if most of your metrics are pulled from an InfluxDB database
Netdata	A plugin-based dashboarding tool that supports push and pull architectures for metric displaying
Kibana	Largely used with Elasticsearch and Logstash to form the ELK stack

Grafana

As Grafana is the most popular tool today, it is worth exploring what Grafana has to offer.

233

What Is Grafana

Grafana is an open source plugin-based dashboarding tool that has a wide range of data source options that can be used to display metrics without duplicating any data. Grafana can be deployed on almost all platforms used today, from Windows through to Debian (Figure 7-8).

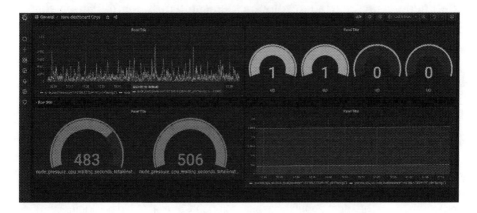

Figure 7-8.

A basic example of a Grafana dashboard can be seen in Figure 7-8.

Using Grafana

There are a few ways to use Grafana:

- Install your own environment on-premise.

- Use the managed Grafana cloud service.

Cloud Service

If you do not want to run your own Grafana instance on-premise, you can run your dashboarding in the cloud. The free forever plan includes Grafana, 10K Prometheus series, 50 GB logs, and more.

On-Premise Installation

Grafana can be deployed in a few ways:

- Manual installation following the official documentation on the Grafana documentation page.

- Use podman to pull a Grafana container image with Grafana prebuilt and run a Grafana container.

Recommendation   Use an automation tool like Ansible and download a prebuilt Ansible role to do the deployment for you.

Data Sources

Before you can create a dashboard, you will need to have a source from where metric data will be pulled. These are your data sources. You will need to create a data source before attempting to create a dashboard. Grafana supports a number of data sources that include some of the following:

- Alertmanager

- AWS CloudWatch

- Azure Monitor

- Elasticsearch

- InfluxDB

- MySQL

- PostgreSQL

- Prometheus

- Jaeger

Dashboard Creation

Once you have your data source, you are ready to start creating dashboards. Grafana has the ability to create many different dashboards, and these can be created from the main Grafana screen when you first log in.

Dashboards can be imported and exported if you wish to download prebuilt dashboards or if you wish to share your configuration.

Panels

Once you have your first dashboard, you will want to start creating your metric visualization. For this, dashboards use panels. Multiple panels can be used to display the metrics of your choice from your preconfigured data source. Each panel has a query editor specific to the data source selected in the panel (Figure 7-9).

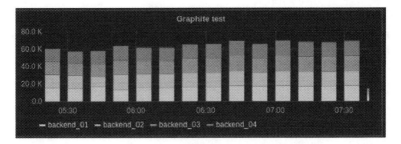

Figure 7-9.

Panels can be duplicated for quick configuration and can be customized to use different colors for your time series data as demonstrated in Figure 7-9.

Rows

To arrange all your panels, you need to create rows; rows are your logical dividers for all your panels. Panels can be dragged into different rows for simple organization.

Save

Always remember to save your dashboards when you have added new panels or rows. If you happen to open a new dashboard, your changes will be lost.

Application Monitoring

A special kind of monitoring that can be a bit more trickier and often more expensive on both resource and time is application monitoring. Application monitoring requires both infrastructure tooling and developers who develop their applications to expose metrics that can be monitored.

Tracing Tools

Tracing tools are used to "trace" the execution path of an application and its transaction by the use of specialized logging. Typically, these are used by developers to aid in pinpointing where a particular issue occurs.

Tracing should not be confused with event monitoring. Event monitoring is primarily used by Linux sysadmins for high-level troubleshooting and is normally not too "noisy." Where, with "tracing" noise is good. The more information, the more accurate the troubleshooting can be to narrow down the root cause.

There are a few tracing tools available today that can be used. Proprietary platforms like AppDynamics are excellent tools with rich features but come with hefty price tags. Fortunately, there are also open source alternatives, and as we are primarily focused on all that is open source, we can just move past those that are not.

Jaeger

Originally open sourced by Uber, Jaeger is inspired by the OpenZipkin and Dapper projects used for monitoring and troubleshooting microservices-based distributed systems. With that, Jaeger promises to help solve the following issues:

- Distributed transaction monitoring

- Performance and latency optimization

- Root cause analysis

- Service dependency analysis

- Distributed context propagation

Zipkin

Before Jaeger, Zipkin was developed as an open source project based on the Google Dapper project. Zipkin is a Java-based application that provides an interface for users to view tracing data from a range of data backends. Zipkin supports transport mechanisms like RabbitMQ and Kafka.

Zipkin can be deployed as a container or run locally by downloading the latest binaries. All of these steps are well documented on the Zipkin official site.

Exposing Metrics

Monitoring tools are only as good as the data they can collect. For standard platform monitoring, the metrics can be pulled using agents which in turn speak to the system they are running on to return the data they need. Applications, however, need to expose the data from within the application so the monitoring agent can pass the data to the monitoring platform. From there, alerts can be configured along with any dashboards.

How to Speak "Developer"

As Linux sysadmins, we need to build monitoring systems that incorporate application metrics; for this, developers need to ensure code is written to expose metrics. The same is true for developing applications that can be traced using tracing software like Jaeger.

Having conversations with developers and building proof of concept applications to show the benefits of tracing along with exposed application metrics is essential when trying to diagnose issues. As your application portfolio grows, having these tools will greatly reduce potential downtime and firefighting. Building these good practices early is well worth the effort than trying to retrofit them later. This may be more difficult if you are using a third party for your application.

Summary

In this chapter, you were introduced to the following:

- What monitoring tools can be run from a standard Linux distro

- Graphical alternative monitoring tools that can be used from a Linux desktop

- What tooling can be used to store historical metric data on a standard Linux distro

- Central monitoring solutions like Nagios, Prometheus, and Thanos

- Enterprise monitoring open source tools such as OpenNMS and CheckMk

- Dashboarding tools that can be used to display metric data in a nice neat manner

- Application monitoring tools used for tracing and how important application metrics are for estate management

CHAPTER 8

Logging

In this chapter, we focus on a topic where we spend most of our time troubleshooting as a Linux sysadmin: logs.

We will explore different logging systems that you can use, how to read logs, how to increase the information we get from logs, and how we look after our systems so logs do not cause us more issues. Finally, we will explore how logs should be offloaded to external logging systems in a neat and secure manner.

Linux Logging Systems

There are a few different options that can be used for system and application logs. By default, all Linux systems are installed with syslog to manage local logs. There are a few alternatives to syslog that can be used, or you can develop your own if you choose.

The two logging systems we will look at briefly are Rsyslog and Fluentd.

Rsyslog

Installed by default on all Linux systems and almost always used, Rsyslog is an incredibly fast logging system with the ability to receive logs from almost everything running on a Linux platform. Rsyslog has the ability to not only receive logs from just about everywhere, it can also offload logs to numerous destinations from files through to MongoDB.

© Kenneth Hitchcock 2022
K. Hitchcock, *Linux System Administration for the 2020s*,
https://doi.org/10.1007/978-1-4842-7984-7_8

Modular

Rsyslog has been designed in a modular way, allowing users to choose what they want to use with rsyslog. There are a number of modules currently available that range from snmp trap configuration through to kernel logging. For a full list of all the different modules you could use, look at the rsyslog official website:

```
www.rsyslog.com/doc/v8-stable/configuration/modules/index.html
```

Installation

If for some very strange reason rsyslog is not installed by default, you can install from your standard package management system, like dnf or apt:

```
# dnf install rsyslog
```

You can also run an rsyslog container if you choose that could be used as a central logging system. More thought will need to be done around storage and connectivity.

Service

The rsyslog service is enabled and started by default but can be stopped or disabled in the standard systemd manner:

```
# systemctl status rsyslog
```

Configuration Files

The configuration files for rsyslog are handled through two configuration locations:

- The overall central configuration file "/etc/rsyslog.conf"

- The ".d" directory for custom configuration files to be stored "/etc/rsyslog.d/"

Rsyslog configuration has three main sections you need to be familiar with:

- Global directives
- Templates
- Rules and actions

Global Directives

General global configuration for rsyslog. Examples include the enabling and disabling of additional modules and library locations.

Templates

Templates give you the ability to format how you want logs to be recorded and allow dynamic file name generation. It's a useful configuration if you are building a central rsyslog system and want to record the hostname of the system sending logs.

Rules

Rules consist of selectors and actions. These are the fields that set what will be logged and where the logs will be sent.

Selector Field

The selector field consists of two parts, the facility and priority. These two parts are divided by the "." character.

The following entries are valid facility types: auth, authpriv, cron, daemon, kern, lpr, mail, news, syslog, user, uucp, and local0 through local7.

The following entries are valid priorities that can be used: debug, info, notice, warning, err, crit, alert, emerg.

The wildcard character of "*" can be used to substitute either or both the facility and priority of the sector field.

Examples of the selector field can be "*.*", "auth.*", and "auth.debug".

Action Field

The action field is typically made up of where the location of the log file will be. However, other actions can also be applied to a particular selector if you choose. Examples of this could be writing to a database or sending the log files to a remote logging system.

Actions can be quite flexible too; different protocols, ports, and interfaces can be configured to send logs to remote systems. It's useful if you run a dedicated logging network to not impact a production network.

Tip   Make use of different selectors to monitor systems for critical errors in separate files. These logs can then be exported to a remote system for immediate alerts on dashboards.

Fluentd

Fluentd is an open source project that was originally created by a company called Treasure Data.

Plugin Based

Written in C and Ruby, Fluentd gives the user the ability to be flexible in how Fluentd can be used. With over 125 plugins for both input and output, Fluentd can be used with almost any system or cloud provider available.

Used at Scale

Running a large-scale environment with Fluentd is entirely possible with user cases reporting that Fluentd can handle over 50,000 systems sending data.

Installation

Fluentd can be installed in a few ways: standard package installation, installed from source, or run from a container.

Prerequisites

Before installing Fluentd, there are a few prerequisites that are required:

- Configure NTP.

- Increase maximum file descriptors to 65535.

- Optimize network kernel parameters for performance-sensitive environments.

- Use sticky bit symlink/hardlink protection.

More information about these prerequisites can be found in the official installation documentation from Fluentd.

Manual Installation

Depending on your system, installing Fluentd can be done by either running a script that matches your distro or installing the required Ruby gems. The recommendation is to use the gem installation for nonsupported platforms, and for supported platforms such as RHEL, to install using the scripts provided by Fluentd.

The official documentation should always be followed for the detailed steps.

Container Deployment

Fluentd can also be deployed as a container and is often deployed in this fashion. The official documentation does highlight all the steps in detail that need to be followed for a successful deployment.

The basic high-level steps are as follows:

1. Pull the Fluentd container image from a reliable or trusted source.

2. Create a basic fluentd.conf configuration file.

3. Run the container and send logs.

Note   There will be more steps than just the preceding steps. Also, don't forget your firewalls.

Configuration

The main configuration file for Fluentd is the fluentd.conf file. Configuration parameters can be found in the official online documentation or man pages. A basic configuration file looks similar to the following:

```
<source>
  @type http
  port 9880
  bind 0.0.0.0
</source>
<match **>
  @type stdout
</match>
```

Understanding Logs

Having logs available is the first step to finding or preventing a problem. Understanding what the logs are actually telling you is another very important step.

Where Are the Log Files

On all major enterprise Linux distros, log files are typically stored in the "/var/log" directory. This directory should normally be mounted on a separate disk partition to avoid the root filesystem from filling if any runaway logging occurs.

Tip   /var/log should always be on a separate partition if you are following any hardening guidelines.

How to Read Log Files

Logs can be viewed with a variety of tools installed on your Linux distro. On a vanilla system, you will at least have access to the "vi" tool, but you can install and use any text editor you are more comfortable with.

Warning   Do not open large log files that are many gigabytes in size using tools like vim on a production system. The file contents will consume large portions of memory and potentially cause you issues. Copy the large logs to a different system to avoid any issues.

Infrastructure Logs

Logs that tell you all about your Linux system's events, services, and system are your infrastructure logs. These logs are the standard logs that are configured in your rsyslog.conf configuration file and tell you all about what your system is doing in the background. These are the logs that will be used to troubleshoot any system issues and can be used to look for issues before they occur.

Important Logs

Logs that should be monitored for system issues are as follows.

/var/log/messages

This log is used to store all the generic events and information about your system. Other distros like Ubuntu or Debian use a log file named syslog instead. This log should always be one of the first places you check if you need to troubleshoot any issues. It may not have all the information but can get you started when you do not know where to begin.

/var/log/secure

This log file is used for authentication events. This log or the /var/log/auth.log in Ubuntu and Debian is the best place to start troubleshooting authentication failures or login attempts.

/var/log/boot.log

This one is fairly straightforward in its purpose. This is used to troubleshoot boot-related issues. It's a useful log to use to see how long a system has been down for.

/var/log/dmesg

This is used to log information about system hardware changes and failures. It's very useful if you are having problems detecting new hardware being added or removed.

/var/log/yum.log

If using a distro that uses yum as its package management system, you can see a history of all packages added, updated, or removed.

/var/log/cron

This is a simple log to capture all cron-related tasks that have run successfully or failed.

Application Logs

Depending on your application or what application server you use, the log files could be stored anywhere. Application developers need to ensure that important information is logged to troubleshoot issues or track events. The ability to increase or decrease verbosity should also be included.

Good Practice

Some good practices for application logging should include the following.

Use /var/log Directory for Logs

Ensure that all logs end up in the /var/log directory, preferably under a subdirectory dedicated for the application. Applications can have their directories symlinked to the /var/log directory if the application is not able to adjust where logs are sent.

Security

Logs that contain sensitive information should be secured when keeping a long history. Permissions to the log directory should be locked to users and groups authorized to read the logs. The use of ACLs could help to keep the logs secure.

Warn or Above

Logs in production should never be left in debug mode. Logs should only be set to warning or error. This will keep the logs small and only report if there is an issue looming or report errors. Setting log levels too low can leave you with your /var/log disk filling up.

Warning   Debugging in production is never a good idea. If the need to do this is frequent, your application is not being tested correctly and should be recommended to not deploy new versions unless rigorously tested.

Increasing Verbosity

When problems occur, there may be a need to get more information than what has been provided.

Log Verbosity Levels

Well-written applications or platforms all tend to have the ability to increase or decrease log verbosity. The following log levels are typically available for users to use when setting logging levels:

- Fatal

- Error

- Warn

- Info

- Debug

- Trace

The default settings for a production application or platform should normally be set to "Warn" or "Error." As previously advised, it is not recommended to debug in production for two reasons:

1. Switching on debugging often requires an application or platform restart, something not easily done while live traffic is on the platform.

2. Debugging will increase the disk usage and add additional load on the system. If the application or platform has a major problem, the debugging logs can grow quickly and potentially fill any logging disks.

However, when the very very rare need does arise, setting the log verbosity to "Debug" will definitely log more information but will be limited to what the application or platform deems as a debugging message. To get the information you need, it is best to start from "Warn" and work down to "Trace" until you have the information you need. Once done, always set the logging level back to "Warn" or "Error."

Log Maintenance

A good Linux sysadmin ensures that all logs are rotated and archived when not being used. A great Linux sysadmin builds log maintenance into all system configuration automation and never has to worry about it again.

If you have never managed logs before, then one of the following is most likely true:

- You have been lucky so far.

- The platform you support does not log enough information for it to be a problem.

- Logs are forwarded to a dedicated logging platform managed by someone else.

Log Management Tools

Logrotate

The first step for any Linux sysadmin when it comes to log maintenance is to configure Logrotate. Logrotate can rotate, compress, and mail log files. Logrotate is managed by the following configuration file and directories:

- /etc/logrotate.conf

  - Used for global configuration

- /etc/logrotate.d

  - Custom configuration files

Installation

Logrotate is installed by default on all enterprise Linux distros and most community distros.

Logrotate provides documentation through its man pages that will give you more than enough information to get started, including examples.

Log Forwarding

Log forwarding is the preferred option for most people today. Enterprise tools like Fluentd are a great way to offload local logs to a central location. It removes the need for local systems to retain logs for extended periods and reduces the disk footprint.

Central Logging Systems

There are a few central logging systems that can be used today, both proprietary and open source. The big names in central logging over the last decade have been Splunk, SolarWinds, Rsyslog, ElasticStack, and Fluentd. The last three are open source and worth spending time to learn about.

Elastic Stack

Also known as ELK stack, Elastic Stack is made up of four tools listed in Table 8-1.

Table 8-1. *Elastic Stack tools*

Tool	Description
Elasticsearch	Used for log analytics and searching
Kibana	A user interface for Elasticsearch
Logstash	Used for log ingestion
Beats	Agents that are used to send logging information to Logstash

Fluentd

Fluentd can be used as a replacement for local logging, as previously discussed in this chapter, and can also be used as a centralized logging platform. To use Fluentd as a central logging platform, you need to have two elements in your network.

Log Forwarders

A log forwarder monitors logs on a local system, filters the information that is required, and then sends the information to a central system. In the case of Fluentd, this would be a log aggregator.

Fluentd has a log forwarder called Fluent Bit which is recommended by Fluentd to use.

An example of a Fluentd forwarder configuration would look similar to the following:

```
<source>
  @type forward
  port 24224
</source>
<source>
  @type http
  port 8888
</source>
<match example.**>
  @type forward
  <server>
    host 192.168.100.1
    port 24224
  </server>
  <buffer>
    flush_interval 60s
  </buffer>
</match>
```

Log Aggregators

The destination for log forwarders would be the log aggregators. They are made up of daemons constantly running and accepting log information to store. The logs can then be exported or migrated to cloud environments for off-site storage.

A Fluentd log aggregate configuration example could look similar to the following:

```
<source>
  @type forward
  port 24224
</source>
# Output
<match example.**>
  # Do some stuff with the log information
</match>
```

Rsyslog

If you do not want to use anything outside of what is provided on a standard enterprise Linux distro, you can stick to using Rsyslog for centralized logging.

Rsyslog Aggregator

Very similar in how Fluentd is configured to use log forwarders and aggregators, Rsyslog can be configured to do the same. Rsyslog can be configured to send and receive logs over either tcp or udp. Rsyslog can also be configured to send and receive logs securely using certificates.

As a minimum for an Rsyslog server to receive logs as a central logging system, you need to ensure the following are in place:

1. Firewall disabled or configured to allow either tcp/udp ports 514 or 6514 depending if you are using the certificate method of forwarding logs.

2. If SELinux is enabled, you will need to configure SELinux to allow rsyslog traffic to log messages to your central system:

    ```
    semanage -a -t syslogd_port_t -p tcp 514
    semanage -a -t syslogd_port_t -p udp 514
    ```

3. Configure NTP.

4. Configure rsyslog.conf to enable modules to receive logs:

    ```
    $ModLoad imtcp
    $InputTCPServerRun 514
    ```

5. Restart the rsyslog service.

Rsyslog Forwarders

To send logs to a central Rsyslog server, you need to also configure the rsyslog.conf file on your Linux client systems to send logs to the central server. A simple configuration to send all logs centrally using tcp is as follows:

```
*.*    @@192.168.0.1:514
```

Note   A single @ is used for udp, whereas two @@ are used to send via tcp.

As with the central Rsyslog server, once the configuration file rsyslog.conf has been updated the rsyslog service will need to be restarted:

```
# systemctl restart rsyslog
```

Summary

In this chapter, you were introduced to the following:

- Different Linux logging systems including how rsyslog can be replaced by Fluentd

- How to understand logs and where to find them

- What the important logs in a Linux system are and what these logs are used for

- Log maintenance and what tools can be used to keep logs from filling up your Linux system

- What can be used to send logs to a central logging system

CHAPTER 9

Security

Security is one of the most important subjects that can be discussed as a Linux sysadmin. All organizations require at least a minimal amount of security to avoid being exposed or sabotaged by random hackers looking for an easy target.

Larger organizations like banks need to focus heavily on security and need to ensure that they are protected at all costs. This will involve ensuring systems are hardened to the nth degree.

This chapter will focus on how security can be enforced and how systems can be checked to ensure they comply not only with good security practices but also meet compliance regulations. In this chapter, we will explore different tools that can be used from the open source community to build secure platforms and how to validate that systems are indeed as secure as possible.

Finally, we will discuss DevSecOps and how the change in culture can improve security. We will look at how today's DevSecOps practices have improved the process in securing Linux systems.

Linux Security

The traditional approach to building and configuring a secure Linux environment would have been to make use of firewalls, SELinux, and in some cases antivirus software.

© Kenneth Hitchcock 2022
K. Hitchcock, *Linux System Administration for the 2020s*,
https://doi.org/10.1007/978-1-4842-7984-7_9

Today, however, we have more than just standard Linux systems deployed in our estates. There are container images, virtual machine images, and cloud instance images, to name a few. How are vulnerabilities checked on these images and how are third-party software checked that are used to run your organization's applications?

How do you as a Linux sysadmin manage these risks in a way that does not stop you from doing your day job? What tools can be used to streamline this process and ensure everything that is released into your estate is secure?

Let's start by looking at the standard Linux security that can be configured on your Linux distros without too much effort. Then look at how cultural change and new tooling can streamline this process for new builds and deployments.

Standard Linux Security Tools

Out of the box, most Linux distros will have tooling installed or be available to install that would allow you to secure the platform to a basic level. The common tools are the firewall, SELinux, and some intrusion detection.

Firewall

The basic description of a Linux firewall is that it is the Netfilter toolset that allows access to the network stack at the Linux kernel module level.

To configure the ruleset for Netfilter, you require a ruleset creation tool. By default, all enterprise Linux systems have a firewall ruleset tool installed, with the exception of certain cloud image versions. These images tend to be more cutdown and do not always include the firewall tooling. This is due to the fact that the protection should be handled at the cloud orchestration layer.

Most Linux distros either have iptables or firewalld installed as their ruleset tool. Both options have a high degree of configuration that can be used to secure your Linux system.

Iptables

Previous Linux distros and a few that have decided to not move forward with systemd still use the firewall ruleset configuration tool known as iptables. Iptables can get complex, but if you have a basic understanding and know how to check if a rule has been enabled, you are well on your way already (Table 9-1).

Table 9-1. *Basic iptables commands*

LVM Command	Description
iptables -L -n	List all rules in all chains in numerical format
iptables --help	Help on what parameters are available
iptables -A INPUT -p tcp --dport 22 -j ACCEPT	Example of adding tcp port 22
iptables -F	Flush all rules from the iptables configuration
iptables-save > /etc/iptables/ rules.v4	Save iptables configuration on Debian/ Ubuntu
iptables-save > /etc/sysconfig/ iptables	Save iptables configuration on RHEL

Firewalld

If you are using an enterprise version of Linux, chances are you most likely will be using systemd. With systemd, you will be using firewalld as the ruleset configuration tool for Netfilter.

Firewalld was designed to be simpler and easier to use than iptables. Firewalld like iptables has a few commands all Linux system administrators should know. Table 9-2 lists some basic commands to remember.

Table 9-2. *Basic firewalld commands*

LVM Command	Description
`firewall-cmd --list-all`	List all rules currently configured
`firewall-cmd --add-port=80/tcp --permanent`	Open tcp port 80
`firewall-cmd --add-service=ssh --permanent`	Open port 22 by referencing the service name
`firewall-cmd --help`	Help
`firewall-cmd --reload`	Reload firewall to enable the new rules

Tip   When possible, use firewall-cmd and never disable the firewall service. Instead, understand what ports are required and open the ports than leaving an entire system open.

SELinux

Another measure of security used on most Linux distros is SELinux, originally conceptualized and worked on by the US National Security Agency.

In summary, SELinux is a Linux kernel security module that allows access to parts of the Linux operating system.

If you imagine your Linux system being a secure building, the outside fencing and walls, gates, main doors, and windows act as your firewall. The inside of the secure building, along with its rooms and facilities, is governed by the on-duty security personnel. It is the job of the security personnel to check who has access to what rooms and what facilities. The security team would, in this case, be acting as SELinux.

Just as you need to understand the basics of your Linux firewall, you too need to understand the basics of SELinux (Table 9-3). For now, all you need to know is how to enable, disable, and restore basic configuration. The more complicated configuration will come with experience.

Table 9-3. *Basic SELinux commands*

LVM Command	Description
getenforce	Display current SELinux state
setenforce 0	Temporarily disable SELinux
setenforce 1	Temporarily enable SELinux
/etc/selinux/config	Configure permanent state of SELinux
restorecon -Rvv /path/ to/file	Restore the SELinux configuration set by current labels on the directory

There are two kinds of intrusion detection that can be used for any server estate: host-based intrusion detection and network-based intrusion detection. For the purposes of this book, we will only discuss what we can deploy on our Linux platforms.

Host-Based Intrusion Detection

Often overlooked and not configured by most Linux sysadmins is some form of host-based intrusion detection. On most Linux enterprise distros, there should at least be one of the following options to install. If not, you may need to install from a community repository like EPEL.

Table 9-4 lists a few options that can be used for host-based intrusion detection.

Table 9-4. *Intrusion detection options*

Tool Name	Description
Aide	The advanced intrusion detection environment is available with standard repositories
Fail2ban	Another popular intrusion detection solution but needs to be installed from EPEL repositories on certain distros
Samhain	Both an integrity checker and host intrusion detection system

Warning   When installing from a community repository, always check with your Linux vendor if they will support the platform if you install third-party tools.

Recommended Linux Security Configurations

If you need to quickly build a Linux system and want to ensure it is as secure as possible, you should at least configure the following.

Disable Root Login

Disable the ability to log in to root through ssh by editing the sshd_config. You will still be able to log in via a console or if you need to rescue your system through single user mode.

Minimal Install

Install your Linux server with the minimal packages selected. It is better to start from a basic build and add the packages you need after. Less is more when it comes to secure Linux server building.

Disk Partitions

Table 9-5 lists all the separate disk partitions that should be configured with the respective mount options.

Table 9-5. *Disk layout and mount options*

Disk	Mount Options
/var	
/var/log	
/var/log/audit	
/var/tmp	Mount to same disk as /tmp
/tmp	nodev, nosuid, noexec
/home	nodev
/dev/shm	nodev, nosuid, noexec
removable media	nodev, nosuid, noexec

Disk Encryption

Only consider the use of disk encryption if the server can easily be taken out of a data center or server room. This would apply to laptops or any portable systems. A common disk encryption tool that can be used is LUKS.

No Desktop

Do not install a Linux desktop or "X Windows System." If it is installed, remove both the desktop and the "X Windows System" packages.

Remember   Set your run level to 3 before attempting to remove packages.

Encrypt Network Communications

Use encrypted communications where possible. Use certificates or keys when opening ssh connections. Mount network filesystems using secure methods without transmitting clear text passwords.

Remove and Disable Insecure or Unused Services

Remove potential insecure packages like telnet or ftp and use secure versions like sftp. It is also recommended to remove or disable unused services.

Apply Updates and Patch Kernel

Sounds obvious, but ensure that your Linux system has been patched to the latest possible level. Upgrade kernels and remove any old kernels once you have confirmed your system is working perfectly with the new kernel.

SELinux and Firewall

Ensure that both SELinux and the Linux firewall are enabled and have the necessary configurations in place.

Improved Authentication Configuration

If you are forced to use local users, configure password aging for Linux user accounts, ensure that no previously used passwords can be used, and lock accounts after failed logins. Finally, ensure that no accounts have empty passwords.

If possible, make use of a central user authentication service like an LDAP server using Kerberos authentication.

Check for Open Ports

Check what ports are currently open and verify if any ports should not be open. A very useful command to check what ports are open on the localhost is as follows:

```
# nmap -sT -O localhost
```

World Writable Files

Check that there are no world writable files or directories. A useful command to check this is as follows:

```
# find /dir -xdev -type d \( -perm -0002 -a ! -perm -1000 \) -print
```

Files Not Owned by Anyone

Any files on a Linux system not owned by anyone can pose a potential security risk. Check for any of the files with the following command:

```
# find /dir -xdev \( -nouser -o -nogroup \) -print
```

ACLs

Configure specific permissions to disks and files using ACLs for users that need access to the system. Do not open system-wide permissions for nonadmin users.

Send Logs to Central Logging Service

Configure all your Linux systems to send logs to a central logging service. This will ensure that you keep track of all login attempts before logs can be wiped.

Intrusion Detection

Install and configure an intrusion detection tool like Aide or Fail2ban. If using Aide, be sure to copy the database to a secure location off the server that is being monitored. This can be used later for comparison purposes.

Application Server Security

If the Linux system will be used as a web server or application server, ensure that certificates are configured for secure communication.

DevSecOps

All these security steps are only as good as the people who apply them. If an organization has not embraced the fact that security is not just the responsibility of the security team, there will be opportunities for the unsavory types out there when a security slip-up occurs. This is why there has to be an evolution in the cultural view of security.

One of the biggest changes in organizations culturally over the last few years has been exactly this. The understanding that everyone is responsible for security.

What Is It?

In the same vein that DevOps is a set of practices and tools designed to bring development and operational teams together by embracing development practices, DevSecOps aims to align everyone within an organization with security practices and tools (Figure 9-1). Basically, it's representing that everyone is responsible for security.

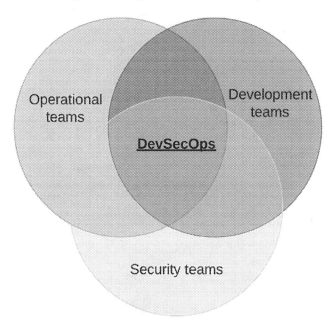

Figure 9-1. *Venn diagram where the different teams meet to create DevSecOps*

Everyone Is Responsible for Security

Just as everyone needs to be vigilant for potential attackers through social engineering and understanding simple security practices for physical security, DevSecOps strives to get everyone thinking about security in all aspects of their technical work.

From deploying new code or building new systems, everything needs to flow through security gates before being released. Pulling third-party content from the Internet needs to be scanned and tested before release.

Security needs to be treated as an evolving entity. Threats need to be detected, and platform remediation needs to be done when problems are found. The process of managing security should follow a similar flow to that shown in Figure 9-2.

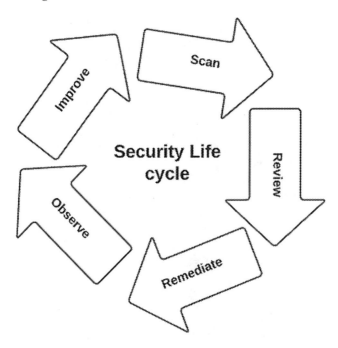

Figure 9-2. *The cycle of security*

Environments are scanned, scans are reviewed, issues are remediated, changes required are observed, and finally the changes are applied to not repeat the issues experienced.

Tools

Linux sysadmins, developers, and users need to be conscious that anything new that is added to a Linux estate must meet security requirements. Running scans and tests manually will not support this cultural shift and will leave you in a position where security is swiped to the side.

All these security checks need to be done in an automated manner. When security issues are detected, the process should be stopped and remediated. If building a new container image, for instance, it is pointless building an insecure container image and wasting storage. It is best to stop, fix the issue, and rerun the build.

Security Gates

One good way to incorporate DevSecOps practices would be to build security gates into pipeline tools such as Jenkins or Tekton (Figure 9-3).

Figure 9-3. *Code is pushed, checked, and baked with a pulled image*

The resulting image that will be used to deploy a new container is checked before being deployed. If the security gate finds a vulnerability, the process is stopped, and the deployment is failed, thus preventing security holes being deployed into a live environment.

Any automation tool could be used to include security gates. Ansible Tower, for instance, has the ability to make use of workflows. Red Hat Satellite or Uyuni has an automated build process that could also be used.

Third-Party Tools

Using third-party tools to scan and check code is highly recommended for your security gates. Using products like SonarQube has the ability to scan for vulnerabilities and check code for syntax issues.

System Compliance

There are numerous reasons for systems to be compliant. The ability to be able to store credit card details for one dictates how systems should be secured within financial organizations. Failure to do so would mean financial penalties or worse.

For systems to be compliant, there are hardening requirements that need to be followed. These requirements need to be applied to all systems and have evidence provided when audit time arises.

System Hardening

Hardening a Linux system is a process of removing any potential attack surfaces your system may have.

There are many areas that a system can be exposed for a would-be attacker to use. For example, a recently discovered vulnerability has been shown to allow a non-root user the ability to exploit a vulnerability in the sudoedit command. This vulnerability allows the user to run privileged commands without authorization.

Finding these kinds of vulnerabilities and remediating them before being exposed is the most important thing we as Linux sysadmins can do. Reducing the chance of the problem happening in the first place is even more important when building hundreds if not thousands of systems. This is why system hardening and system vulnerability scanning are vital to ensuring your systems are as secure as possible before going live.

Hardening Standards

There are a number of standards that can be used today to harden your Linux estate. The two main ones used are CIS and STIGs. Both are very similar, largely due to the fact that there are only so many security tweaks one can do. Both, however, do serve as a good starting point to secure your platforms to a good standard.

There are a few other standards that must also be followed for different organizations such as NIST 800-53 for US federal agencies and PCI DSS for financial organizations or anyone that wants to store credit/debit card details. These standards are typically applied over and above the STIGs or CIS guidelines.

Center for Internet Security

If you have spent any time doing system hardening in the past, you may already be familiar with CIS standards. CIS is a nonprofit organization aiming to keep the connected world as secure as possible. CIS provides their security guides for free to anyone who needs them and also provides a paid-for service where CIS can provide already hardened resources like system images.

As Linux sysadmins, it is enough to download the hardening guides and follow the steps to securing your platform. The guides are quite well written; they explain what the security configuration is for and how to remediate your platform if found to be vulnerable. The guides even give you the commands to run.

In the past, I have written shell scripts by copying and pasting the commands from these guides. Today, there are much better ways of doing this, which I will cover shortly in this chapter.

Security Technical Implementation Guides

Very much like CIS, there are STIG guides you can follow to harden your platforms too. These guides are also available for free but are a bit more structured with US government requirements more in mind.

STIG guides are also not as varied as CIS guides. STIG guides may not have guides for community-based platforms or applications compared to CIS. The use of generic guides would have to be used where CIS has dedicated guides that can be used.

Hardening Linux

There are a few ways to harden your Linux systems.

Manual Configuration

The last way I would ever harden a Linux system would be by doing it manually. The sheer number of hardening steps that need to be followed would keep you busy till the cows come home. Most hardening guides are well over 100 pages long and are far from a riveting read.

If the need arose that a system had to be hardened by hand, then the best tool you could follow would be the hardening guides available on the Internet like CIS.

Each of the different hardening guides available all comes with commands to determine if a system is vulnerable and, if the vulnerability is in fact present, also provides the remediation commands. Your friend in this case would be to copy and paste until you have got to the end of the extensive guide.

My advice would be to push back as hard as possible on doing anything manually. The time it would take would far exceed what time it would take to set up the next method of hardening a system.

Automation

Automation is your friend. The Internet is awash with content written by Linux sysadmins like you that need to harden systems. Chances are you will find some Ansible or Puppet that will do exactly what you want. You also will have the added benefit of the process being repeatable, which could be very handy when your boss tells you to harden another five systems.

Tip   Remember to search those Internet resource galaxies like Ansible Galaxy or Puppet Forge for content.

OpenSCAP

Where Internet-downloaded automation might fail you slightly is if you need to replicate configuration from a different already hardened system. There may be a particular system that has specific hardening that does not have all hardening applied for a good reason.

How would you then go about running your standard hardening to accommodate the same settings?

For this use case, you can make use of OpenSCAP. OpenSCAP has the ability to scan a system or systems and generate a report of the system's configuration. This configuration can be compared to another system, and a subsequent report can be run to list the differences.

The absolutely amazing thing about OpenSCAP is that it can also generate Ansible or Puppet code to remediate the differences for you, saving you from having to write your own automation.

OpenSCAP can be run with CIS profiles out of the box and can also use other profiles. Most if not all will present you with the remediation of vulnerabilities through Ansible or Puppet.

OpenSCAP will require you to have the OpenSCAP workbench tool installed on the Linux desktop to allow you to configure profiles.

Tip   Before starting to write automation code, check if OpenSCAP cannot do it for you.

Vulnerability Scanning

Keeping an eye on your estate and ensuring that there are no vulnerabilities is vital to ensuring that you do not have any nasty surprises waiting.

Linux Scanning Tools

OpenVAS

A tool many system administrators would have heard about at some point in their career is Nessus. OpenVAS is a fork of Nessus before Nessus became close sourced by Tenable. OpenVAS (Open Vulnerability Assessment System) is the scanner component of a larger set of tools called Greenbone Vulnerability Manager.

OpenVAS also obtains the tests required to detect vulnerabilities from a live feed that has a good history and gets updated daily.

OpenSCAP

OpenSCAP is another very good vulnerability scanning tool that is more than just a scanning tool as previously discussed. OpenSCAP has the ability to use multiple profiles and can be fully customized to scan based on your organization's requirements.

ClamAV

If you need an open source antivirus, ClamAV can assist with the detection of viruses, trojans, and many other types of malware. ClamAV can be used to scan personal emails or files for any malicious content. ClamAV can also serve as a server-side scanner.

The "paid-for" ClamAV product does an automatic and regular update of its database, in order to be able to detect recent threats. The community product requires some further configuration with cron jobs.

Container Image Scanning Tools

Running Linux estates today requires the management of more than standard Linux systems. Containers and the images they are built from need to be scanned for vulnerability just the same as standard Linux systems.

Harbor

Technically, a container image repository. Harbor is an open source project that provides role-based access to its container registry with the ability to scan images for vulnerabilities. VMware has adopted Harbor as their container registry for their Tanzu Kubernetes platform.

Role-Based Access

Harbor secures artifacts with policies and role-based access control, ensuring images are scanned and free from vulnerabilities.

Trivy

Harbor prior to version 2.2 used Clair as its vulnerability scanner but has since moved on to use Trivy. Harbor can also be connected to more than one vulnerability scanner. By connecting Harbor to more than one scanner, you widen the scope of your protection against vulnerabilities.

Single or Multiple Images

Harbor can be initiated to scan a particular image or on all images in the Harbor environment. Policies can also be set to automatically scan all images at specific intervals.

JFrog Xray

JFrog Xray is a vulnerability scanning tool provided by JFrog. Xray is natively integrated with Artifactory to scan for vulnerabilities and software license issues. Xray is able to scan all supported package types from binaries to container images.

Deep Scanning

Deep scanning allows Xray to scan for any threats recursively through dependencies of packages or artifacts in Artifactory, before being released for live deployments.

Clair

Clair (from a French term that means clear) is an open source project which offers static security and vulnerability scanning for container images and application containers.

Supported Images

The currently supported images that Clair can scan for vulnerabilities include all the major enterprise distros discussed in this book. They are as follows:

- Ubuntu

- Debian

- RHEL

- SUSE

- Oracle

Clair also supports the following images that are being used today in different environments:

- Alpine

- AWS Linux

- VMware Photon

- Python

Enterprise Version

Clair is currently the vulnerability scanning tool that is used within the Red Hat Quay (pronounced "kway" not "key") product. Clair provides an enterprise-grade vulnerability scanning tool for the Red Hat supported container registry.

Continuous Scanning

Clair scans every image pushed to Quay and continuously scans images to provide a real-time view of known vulnerabilities in your containers.

Dashboard

Clair too has a detailed dashboard showing the state of container images stored within Quay.

Pipeline

Working in DevSecOps methodology, the Clair API can be leveraged in pipeline tooling like Jenkins or Tekton to scan images being created during the baking phase.

Container Platform Scanning Tools

Red Hat Advanced Cluster Security for Kubernetes (StackRox)

One of the more recent acquisitions to Red Hat has been the inclusion of StackRox into Red Hat's portfolio. StackRox currently is the upstream project for the Red Hat ACS product but continues to have a community version available for nonsupported platforms.

Red Hat's enterprise equivalent of StackRox provides the following features.

Vulnerability Scanning

The ability to find and fix vulnerabilities in containers running within Kubernetes or OpenShift platforms.

Compliance Scanning

Supported by informative dashboarding, Red Hat ACS can scan containers and images to ensure they meet compliance requirements from standards like CIS, PCI, or NIST, to name a few examples.

Network Segmentation

Ability to enforce network policies and tighter segmentation of allowed network traffic in and out of Kubernetes or OpenShift environments.

Risk Profiling

All risks detected from deployments within Kubernetes or OpenShift can be viewed in a priority list for remediation.

Configuration Management

Used to not only manage the security and vulnerabilities of container workload within Kubernetes or OpenShift. Red Hat ACS can also harden the cluster components through the configuration management.

Detection and Response

By using a combination of rules, allowlists, and baselining, Red Hat ACS is able to identify suspicious activity and take action to prevent attacks.

Falco

Created by Sysdig, Falco is another open source threat detection solution for Kubernetes and OpenShift type environments. Falco can detect any unexpected behaviors in applications and alerts you about the threats in runtime.

Falco has the following features.

Flexibly Rules Engine

By using syntax similar to tcpdump, Falco can build rules using the libscap and libsinsp libraries to pull data from Kubernetes/OpenShift API servers or container runtime environments. Rules can then be created from metadata on specific namespaces or container images.

Immediate Alerting

Reduce risk to your estate with immediate alerts allowing quicker remediation of vulnerabilities.

Current Detection Rules

Up-to-date detection rules based on the latest CVEs or known vulnerabilities. As soon as the security platform knows of a vulnerability, so will you.

Aqua Security

Aqua Security is designed to protect applications that are built using cloud-native containers and being deployed into hybrid cloud infrastructure like Kubernetes or OpenShift.

Aqua Security has the following features.

Developer Guidance

Aqua Security guides developers in building container images that are secure and clean by ensuring they don't have any known vulnerabilities in them. Aqua Security even checks that the container images being developed do not have any known passwords or secrets and any kind of security threat that could make those images vulnerable.

Informative Dashboarding

Aqua Security has a clear and useful dashboard that provides real-time information about the platform being managed with all the issues discovered. If any vulnerability is found, Aqua Security reports the issues back to the developer with recommendations on what is required to fix the vulnerable images.

Summary

In this chapter, you were introduced to the following:

- Standard Linux security tools that should be used and never disabled

- Linux configuration that should be used as a minimum when securing a new system

- The understanding of what DevSecOps is and how this new practice needs to be embraced by everyone within an organization

- System compliance and Linux hardening

- Guides that can be used to harden Linux systems to meet compliance requirements

- Vulnerability scanning tools

CHAPTER 10

Maintenance Tasks and Planning

Any Linux sysadmin will be familiar with the dreaded maintenance required for Linux estates. In this chapter, we will discuss the various maintenance jobs that should be done when managing a Linux estate. We will look at what actual maintenance work should be done, when the maintenance jobs should be run, and how to plan maintenance to cause the least amount of downtime.

This chapter will also briefly look at how maintenance tasks and bureaucratic tasks can be synced to reduce the overall pain that routine maintenance can sometimes bring. Finally, we will discuss how automation should be used to improve the overall maintenance experience for everyone involved.

What Maintenance Should Be Done

There are a number of checks that should be done on a Linux server. Some may not need to be done each maintenance cycle, but some will need to be done as often as possible. There may even be times you need to run emergency maintenance.

© Kenneth Hitchcock 2022
K. Hitchcock, *Linux System Administration for the 2020s*,
https://doi.org/10.1007/978-1-4842-7984-7_10

Note   To determine if maintenance is critical, pay attention to your monitoring for signs of potential issues looming. Examples of this could be disks getting close to being filled up.

Patching

The number one reason for maintenance will be patching and system updates. It cannot be stressed how important this process is and should never be neglected. Patching not only contains package updates and fixes but also provides vulnerability remediation.

Staging

It is never a good idea to patch your production/live or customer-facing environments before confirming that nothing will break with the current round of updates.

This is why a staged approach to patching should always be taken. Determine the order in which you want to patch your environments and patch them in stages.

Figure 10-1 is an example of a patching order I have typically used in the past.

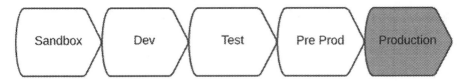

Figure 10-1. *Patching order*

Sandbox

Start with a sandbox type environment with at least one system that runs similar or close to the same applications as your production environment. This environment should not be user facing or require change control approval to work on. The entire environment should be disposable and automated. Sandbox is your environment and is there to prove configuration will not cause issues in other environments.

Automated Testing

If possible, make use of automated testing to prove updates or patch configuration has not broken functionality of your test application. There are numerous options available both open source and proprietary that can be used to automate application testing. Speak to your organization's developers or reach out to who provides your applications. They will more than likely give you recommendations on what you should use.

Here are some options you can also look into that could help:

- Selenium

- Katalon Studio

- Appium (for mobile applications)

- Robotium

Automated Patching

If your patching process is well planned and platform testing can be automated, there really is little stopping you from automating your actual patching grunt work.

Make use of automation tooling like Ansible Tower or Jenkins or anything that allows you to run stages or workflows. This way, you are able to run the following in stages:

- Prechecks

- Confirm failovers have occurred

- Patch operating system files

- Reboots

- Automated testing

Rollback

Pipelines or workflow tooling can also apply rollbacks if problems are detected, ensuring when the maintenance window closes, nothing is left in a problematic state. Automation is great, but building in as much risk management is going to save you having to explain why an environment was broken by your automation.

Hint   You want to make sure you have as much risk reduction in place to ensure your automation is not blamed for system outages. This is what makes your life easier and should be safeguarded from the naysayers.

Filesystem

One area that can grow and cause concern over time if not well maintained is your filesystems. Filesystems not only store logs, they also store files users leave behind in their home directories. Paying attention to your filesystems before they become a problem is crucial to not having preventable outages.

Cleanup

During your system maintenance, it is definitely worth running through the following different filesystems and checking if there are any files that are no longer required. Removing these files and any temporary files are recommended.

Check for Errors

Once you have checked for unused files and cleared as much as possible, it is well worth running a filesystem health check. This will help identify any possible underlying issues before they become a problem further down the line.

Filesystem Check Commands

The commands in Table 10-1 are very useful when running filesystem maintenance or generally looking to resolve disk issues.

Table 10-1. *Basic filesystem check commands*

Linux Command	Description
du -k /var/log | sort -n | tail -10	Check for the ten largest files in a directory
find . -type f -size +100M -ls	Find any files in the current directory larger than 100MB
find /var/log -mtime +90 -ls -exec rm {} \;	Find any files older than 90 days and remove them
tar -zcvf var_log.`date +%Y%m%d`.tar.gz /var/log/*.log	Create a tar file of all the log files in the /var/log directory

Firewall

Firewall checks are just there to ensure no unexpected new rules have made their way into your Linux system. Technically, these should be managed by configuration management tools, but in the case when you do not have a running SaltStack or Puppet, checking the firewall is a quick and simple task. Doing it during a maintenance window just means you can remove any unwanted changes, provided you are covered by any change control.

Important   Firewall rules should always be recommended by internal architects who have designed the platform. If any rules have appeared that don't make sense, refer back to the original designs to confirm they should be there.

Backups

This one really goes without saying. Backups should be done for any systems that cannot be rebuilt from code and done within acceptable time frames. Virtual machines can be backed up in their entirety, but physical systems will need to have specific directories backed up based on the function of the server.

During your maintenance window, double-check that all backups have been running and that a recent backup is in place.

Important   Before patching or doing anything to your system that could leave you in a down state, ensure that you have a recent backup to restore from.

How often your estate should have maintenance done will depend on a few factors:

1. How often do you wish to patch your environment?

2. Do you have problems with disks filling up or disks getting corrupt?

3. Do you have unexpected configurations appearing on your platforms?

Two of the preceding points would indicate you have bigger problems in your estate than maintenance; dealing with those first would be the recommendation before trying to solve symptoms.

As Often As Possible

The obvious task that should be done on a regular basis is patching. Patch cycles depend on the organization's policies, which could be every 7 days or every 90 days. Ninety days is far too long in my opinion and should be pushed down to a minimum of 30 days, but that too is a bit long.

If you were given the decision to make, I would recommend patching as often as possible. Automation should be used and should help reduce the human factor with regular maintenance. By running very regular maintenance and patching, you reduce any possible risk posed by a newly discovered vulnerability.

No Live Patching Without Testing

Regular patching will also allow you to use a staged approach to your patching process, thus reducing possible issues with untested configuration or updates.

Structure

By having a regular maintenance window for each environment, you can plan and structure how updates are applied and tested. Doing this, you drastically reduce the possibility of issues in your live environments both from bugs and vulnerabilities.

How Should Maintenance Be Done

Quite simple, automated maintenance is the way forward today. The human factor needs to be reduced in how we maintain and build our platforms. This is the only way you can truly scale. Having one person or a team of people running maintenance is crazy, let alone if maintenance is going to be done on a regular basis like it should be done.

Automation

I'm sure I mentioned automation enough times now for you to be sick of the term, and I'm also fairly confident most of you are already automating by now.

To state the obvious, automating maintenance is about as important as automating your build process. The following are items you should be automating:

- Backups

- Patching

- Disk cleanup

- Disk checking

- Firewall and SELinux configuration

- Software removal

A few of the preceding items should be managed by configuration management tools, but if you are not using any, then your maintenance automation should take care of them.

Your automation should also be run in a similar order to the following:

1. Check and confirm a recent backup has been taken.

2. Apply any system updates.

3. Run automated testing to confirm updates have not broken anything.

4. Disk cleanups.

5. Configuration checks.

6. Roll back updates if testing failed.

7. Update monitoring or generate reports to reflect status.

Zero Downtime Environments

If your environments are regarded as critical and can afford zero downtime, you will need to be running either multiple data centers or multiple environments per site in a blue/green style deployment.

Blue/Green

This method would involve switching traffic to either blue or green and then patching the nonlive environment.

The blue/green approach does give you the ability to update directly into your live environments if you wish, as you technically are not updating the "live" side. Provided you do all your due diligence and ensure the environment you are patching is 100% running before switching back, you should never experience an outage.

Once you have completed maintenance on one side, you can apply the same maintenance to the second. As you have already proven there to be no issue, you should be perfectly ok to proceed with your second site.

I would personally still recommend taking a staged approach, but if you are pressed for time, you do at least have the protection of your second environment you can switch back to.

Failover

Running multiple data centers is another common approach to reducing single points of failure. Failing your live traffic to your second data center will allow maintenance to happen with zero downtime to live traffic.

The same principles of maintenance should apply before failing back to your primary data center and patching your secondary site.

Maintenance Planning

The execution is only as good as the plan. There are a couple of important things to consider for any maintenance planning.

Agree Maintenance Window

Find a regular time slot for maintenance per environment. Automate the bureaucratic red tape to ensure maintenance can run in these regular times. By finding and planning a known time slot with your organization, you will always be able to apply updates and changes without needing to argue why each time.

This does not mean you have to run maintenance each time, you just have the freedom to do it when required.

If you have automated the process, then even better. Your environment can then constantly stay up to date and run as smoothly as possible, reducing the need to constantly fix issues and allowing you more time to focus on the more exciting things.

Bite-Size Chunks

If you have a large amount of maintenance to do and have not automated the process yet, break your maintenance down into bite-size chunks. Rather run multiple small maintenance windows than one large window.

Remember   Tired eyes help no one.

Art of Estimating

Be careful how you calculate the time required to complete a task. Rather overestimate and finish early than underestimate and put yourself under pressure. Speak to other Linux sysadmins for help on estimating time when planning.

Automating Process and Task Together

Automation is not only about technical task implementation. Today, it is possible to automate the "red tape" processes within your organization too.

In the case of system maintenance, this functionality can be nicely tied with task automation. All the approvals can be automated and fed into your technical automation platform to go ahead when the maintenance window arrives. Not only do you not have to do the manual technical implementations anymore, you can also avoid doing the bureaucratic work.

Process Automation

There are a few different products and projects available today to assist you in automating processes, but one worth mentioning is Red Hat Process Automation Manager, or PAM.

Red Hat PAM

Red Hat PAM provides the tooling to automate business processes and decisions. By using advanced business rules and process engines, along with complex event processing and case management, Red Hat PAM can help solve complex planning and scheduling problems. PAM utilizes the full capabilities of Drools, a powerful and widely used open source rules engine. PAM can even assist in solving complex optimization problems, by using the built-in solver tool.

Like most other Red Hat products, the upstream project for Red Hat PAM is the jBPM project, a fully open source product that can be used with community support.

Warning   Red Hat PAM is the tool you will need to use to develop your process tasks, just as you would with Ansible when automating technical tasks.

Summary

In this chapter, you were introduced to the following:

- What Linux system maintenance needs to be done

- When Linux maintenance should be run

- Methods of running maintenance with zero downtime

- How to plan Linux maintenance

- How to automate maintenance processes and technical tasks together

PART IV

See, Analyze, Then Act

Troubleshooting and asking for help are probably the most important skills a good Linux sysadmin should have in their armory. Most of us learn these skills through trial and error with experience or hopefully through the experience of others with books like mine. The following chapters show you how to approach and solve difficult problems.

CHAPTER 11

Troubleshooting

Troubleshooting can be a difficult skill to master if you do not understand the correct approach. Just digging through logs or configuration files may help resolve simple issues, but understanding how to find the root cause of an issue is where the real skill comes. In this chapter, we will look at how a problem should be looked at, how the problem should be analyzed, and finally how you should act on the information you have seen. Taking your time to understand before guessing is paramount to solving your problem quicker and more efficiently.

Once we have been through how a problem should be approached, we will discuss the proper etiquette that should be used when asking questions in the community. Learning to not ask others to do your work for you or at least framing your questions in such a manner that it seems like you have at least tried is the first step. In this chapter, we will go through the best way to go about asking for help.

Finally, we will address the not so good ways of troubleshooting that you should try to avoid.

See, Analyze, Then Act

The art to becoming an effective troubleshooter is to become an investigator. Follow the clues and ask the right questions. Pay attention to every small detail and most importantly understand why the problem

© Kenneth Hitchcock 2022
K. Hitchcock, *Linux System Administration for the 2020s*,
https://doi.org/10.1007/978-1-4842-7984-7_11

occurred in the first place. Too often, bandages are applied to symptoms, and the underlying issues are not fixed. Fix the root cause and you save yourself all the pain later.

Understand the Problem

To fully understand how to fix a problem, you need to understand what the effects of the problem are; this will most likely give you your first clue as to where to start looking.

To effectively problem-solve, you need to understand what you are troubleshooting, pointless guessing if you don't know how it all works in the first place. You will only get part of the answer and potentially end up wasting time looking for the answer in the wrong place.

If you have a network issue, for instance, but have no idea how to trace network traffic, you are better off getting someone who does know to work with you on the issue. Learning as you go is how we gain experience, so don't be afraid to ask for help. Just do it properly; we will cover that shortly.

Know Where to Start

Knowing where to start is half the battle to get you to the bottom of the issue. Starting from the top sounds like a cliché, but it is how you work your way through the evidence to follow the breadcrumbs that will eventually lead you to the root cause.

Asking the right questions in the beginning will give you ideas where to start digging. When issues are described as "it's broken" or "it's down," it means your questions need to be simple to start with, then become more complex as you dig further. Remember to base your questions on the knowledge level of the people you are working with and to be patient.

Standard Questions to Ask When Starting

When you are new to a problem, you need to understand the problem from the perspective of the person who reported the issue. For that, you should ask your standard questions we all learned in IT school. Questions similar to the following:

- Can you show me what is happening?

- Is the problem repeatable or intermittent?

- Has anything changed?

Note   There is nothing wrong with asking yourself these questions. If anything, it may allow you to deepen your understanding of the issue.

Explain the Problem

When a problem is complex, it requires deep thought, questioning, and understanding. Only through explanation does it become clearer. By going through multiple sessions of explaining and questioning, you increase your knowledge of the problem until you get your answer.

Here are some techniques you can use to explain your problem.

Explain to Yourself

We have known for decades that explaining a problem to ourselves can greatly increase our chances of solving it. By explaining the problem to yourself, you gain new knowledge about the issue, you ask yourself questions, and you challenge yourself to what you understand about the issue. Speak aloud to yourself if it helps and continue to talk to yourself about the issue. Don't stew in silence, find a quiet room if you have to, and thrash out the issue.

Rubber Duck

If after explaining the problem to yourself you still don't have something tangible, grab an inanimate object (rubber duck) and explain your problem to it. Just the process of explaining for a second time may help.

Another Person

If the rubber duck option fails, try explaining your problem to another person; they don't even have to be technical. In fact, it may be better if they are not. This will allow you to simplify your explanation so they understand and possibly in the process help you uncover something you may have overlooked because it was so simple.

Use Tools

Using a whiteboard or scrap paper when explaining will also allow you to get the ideas and thoughts out of your head. Rereading the explanation back to yourself may add further clarity.

Break Down the Problem

Complex problems will involve many different moving parts. Understanding these parts piece by piece will not only give you more clarity about the problem but will also allow you to start eliminating possible causes.

Break the problem down to the individual parts and start explaining to yourself what these parts do, ask if the problem could exist within each part, and then eliminate what could not be the problem.

Using a whiteboard or piece of paper is a great way of visualizing your problem at the different components.

Onions, They Have Layers

While you are breaking down the problem, remember to consider all the layers involved. If you are experiencing an application issue, look at everything from the application down to the physical hardware. By eliminating all the impossible, you are left with the most probable.

The Five Whys

While not everyone likes to talk to themselves or involve inanimate objects, there is another similar way you can use to approach troubleshooting complex issues: a technique called the five "whys."

In this approach, the troubleshooter goes through five questions as to why something has gone wrong.

Example

If we take a scenario where your organization's internal intranet won't load after the evening maintenance, the "whys" shown in Figure 11-1 can be asked.

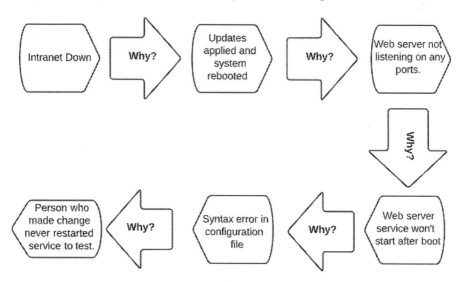

Figure 11-1. *Example of the flow that whys should follow when trying to determine an underlying issue*

The intranet is down. Why? Updates were applied and the system rebooted. Why? The web server was not listening on any ports. Why? The web server service will not start after boot. Why? There's a syntax error in the configuration file. Why? The final why is what brings you to your root cause. Someone had made a change to the web server configuration and did not test the syntax. The change was never applied by restarting the web service, and only when the web server was rebooted after system updates were applied did the true problem manifest itself.

In this example, the problem was down to an undocumented change that happened to the intranet web server. The change was never tested in a syntax check, and the service was never restarted to apply the change. After the server updates and reboot, the web server tried to start on boot but failed due to a syntax error.

Theorize Based on Evidence

During the journey of troubleshooting difficult or intermittent issues, you may need to come up with different avenues of where to investigate. Each avenue will need to be investigated and require evidence to prove it is the smoking gun before the fix can be applied to the affected live environment.

Hypothesis Building

The workflow shown in Figure 11-2 can help with your root cause analysis by building a series of hypotheses.

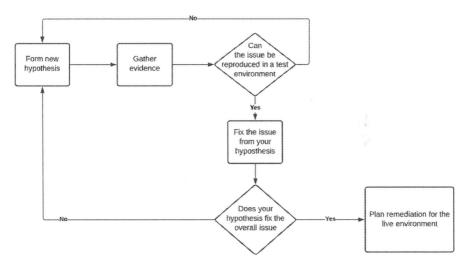

Figure 11-2. *Flow that should be followed when building a troubleshooting hypothesis*

Tip   Before building your hypothesis, don't be too quick to discount the improbable unless you know 100% for sure it cannot be the problem.

Build Your Theory

A good theory should always start with a good hypothesis or an educated guess. To test the hypothesis, all the information about the suspected area needs to be gathered. This could include configuration files, system load, memory usage, or anything that could help you reproduce the issue experienced in the live environment.

Causality

When building your hypothesis, avoid falling into a trap of not understanding the cause and effect of a component, for example, blaming the kernel version because a new graphics card failed to load. Even though the kernel is responsible for device drivers, it still requires the driver from the hardware manufactured compiled in the kernel.

Prove Your Theory

As debugging and testing in a live environment is never a good idea, your theory will need solid evidence to back your claim before you can apply anything to a live environment. For this reason, you need to prove your theory.

Reproduce the Issue

To prove your theory, you first must reproduce the issue. With your evidence gathered, you must try to replicate the same conditions as the live environment and see if you can experience the same issues. If you cannot reproduce the issue, it is possible you have the wrong theory, or you have not gathered all the evidence.

Fix in the Test Environment

If you are able to reproduce the issue, you can test your potential fix and prove the problem has been resolved. The whole process should ideally be repeatable.

Remediation

Finally, with your theory proved and a solution prepared, the live environment can be remediated with little to no risk.

Ask for Help

Early in my career, I was told to always ask for help and not to waste more time than what was required to solve a problem. If I was stuck, I should not "bash my head" for too long before asking. After all, we all are still learning; we work in an industry that is constantly moving and changing. Someone sitting next to you or on the Internet may already have experienced the same problem you have and may have the answer you may be struggling with.

What to Do Before Asking for Help

When you ask for help, you are asking someone to give up some of their time to help you with your problem. The person helping you has to spend energy understanding your problem; they need to think of a possible solution they may have used in the past and then try to explain it to you in a way you can understand.

For that effort, you as the requester should have at least done the following before you even asked the question:

- Tried to fix the problem and failed

- Read the documentation supplied by the software or hardware vendor

- Searched the Internet for examples of what others have tried and checked that no one has already asked the question you want help on

Training

If you are fortunate enough to have access to training materials, check if there is anything you may have been taught in exercises that could assist.

If you never had any training, speak to your organization's manager to get you on appropriate training courses. Failing that, there are plenty of online resources you can also make use of to learn.

How to Ask for Help

The following are some very important points you need to consider when asking for help.

Proper Grammar

Use proper grammar and spelling where possible. If English is not your first language, then do the best you can and start your question with something similar to this:

"I am sorry for my bad English, I hope my question makes sense."

Try to avoid using slang and use the proper spelling of words where possible. Remember you are asking for help, make sure your question is as clear as it can be.

Spelling

Spell-check your questions using whatever tool you have available. Google Docs has decent spell-checking (I hope, as this book was written in it), and it's free.

Either write or copy your question to a new document and check for both grammar and spelling mistakes.

How to Phrase Your Questions

Now with the use of correct spelling and grammar understood, you need to understand the importance of how your questions should be phrased.

Simply asking "Does anyone know why my graphics card does not work on my Linux desktop?" is not enough or well written.

Asking a question that prompts people to immediately ask you for more details is not going to get you the answer you want or any answer at all.

Changing your question to include the following bits of information will get you a much better response:

- State what you have tried.

- Give the details of all the components, like the make and model of the graphics card. Tell the readers what Linux distro you are using.

- Explain that you have read documentation and been through other examples.

- Be very specific about your issue in the main body of your question and give a single line on top summarizing your problem.

A Better Question

Radeon RX 5700xt driver will not work with Fedora 34

I am currently trying to install the Radeon RX 5700XT graphics card in my fresh install of Fedora 34. After reading the official documentation on the AMD site and checking the help of the install command, I am still not able to find a solution.

I have tried running the commands

./amdgpu-install-pro --opencl=pro,legacy

and ./amdgpu-install-pro --opencl=rocr,legacy
but both give me the error.
"Cannot find device"
Here is the output of my log file.
"Log files entries"

Any help would be greatly appreciated or any documentation you may have that I may have missed would also be very helpful.

Tip   Do not rush your question; take time to ask the question in a clear and nonvague manner. People will respond to a question that has been asked by someone who took the time and effort to ask correctly.

Where to Ask Questions

How to ask questions is vital to getting a positive response, but where to ask the correctly worded questions is equally important.

Correct Area

People really do not like being asked questions about subjects that are not relevant to the area you are asking your question in. Make sure you select the correct forum or chat room or even support email before you ask your question.

The general polite response will redirect you to the correct place, but someone with less patience may pass a slightly more sarcastic answer. So do avoid embarrassment or at least wasting your time. Ask your questions where they should be asked.

Forums

If you have a problem with a particular product or project, check if they have a forum you can ask questions on. Be sure to first check if your question has not already been asked.

GitHub, Stack Overflow

There are numerous sites where you can ask technical questions around anything you may be struggling with. Stack Overflow is a common site where I find answers, but places like GitHub can also offer some good insights.

Support Cases

If your problem is around an enterprise product that you or your organization is paying subscriptions for, raise a support case with their help desks. This is after all what you are paying for.

Be sure however to be very clear on what your problem is. Attach log files and potentially diagnostic outputs where possible. Just by adding all the relevant files, you can sometimes get your problem solved quicker.

Things to Avoid When Troubleshooting

Troubleshooting is usually something we don't do for fun; it normally has time pressure associated with it for you to resolve the problem as soon as possible.

To avoid wasting time, there are a few things you should always try to avoid.

Live Debugging

Do not debug in live environments; anyone who says that live debugging is ok is treading on very thin ice. All it takes is one syntax error or one configuration file to be left in debug mode to cause an outage.

There is a reason why test environments and nonproduction environments are built. Use them to find the root cause, not your live environment.

Correlation vs. Causation

When you are looking for the root cause of your problem, focus on where the issue could possibly lie by applying logical thinking. Break down the problem from components that could potentially be responsible, and avoid focusing on components that rely on the possibly faulty components. Basically, avoid wasting time on areas that could be a victim of the root cause and not the cause of it.

With the case of a service not starting, do not waste your time looking at the service file if you have not checked the application configuration first. I am not saying don't check the service file for syntax issues or potential changes, just do not prioritize it.

Being a Lone Wolf

Do not suffer in silence; ask for help and work in pairs. Two sets of eyes are always going to be better than one. Two brains think differently and will approach problems from different angles. Do not spend hours fighting alone.

Guessing and Lying

This is really related to troubleshooting with a group. If you are responsible for something that has happened and you have asked for help to get you out of a jam, be 100% honest and do not guess where you possibly made a mistake.

Owning up to a mistake will often just be treated as just that, "a mistake." Lying about the problem and causing delay with your lack of honesty will most likely not end well for you. Embrace your blunder and learn from it.

Ghosts

Not everyone understands the term "red herring," but it is a term we use in the UK to refer to something that does not exist. A phantom. Avoid looking for something that is unlikely to be the root cause of your problem. Keep applying logical thinking when you are hunting your root cause.

All the Small Things

Do not think all big problems have big causes. Do not forget to check simple things like DNS or has the disk filled up?

Often, it is the things we least expect that can cause the biggest issues; stick to basics and work up from there.

Keep Track of What You Have Tried

Albert Einstein said, "the definition of insanity is doing the same thing over and expecting different results." Nothing is further from the truth when it comes to troubleshooting. If you have a forgetful nature, keep a log of where you checked and the results. This way, you will avoid repeating yourself and wasting time.

Measure Twice, Cut Once

This old saying is true for applying solutions too. Applying dirty workarounds for the sake of getting things to work instantly but later having to fix the same issue in a short period of time is a fool's errand. Finding the root cause and applying a permanent fix should be your first priority.

If your live environment is down, you should ideally be running in your disaster recovery site or within your secondary site. If this is not the case, then there are larger problems than an outage I would be concerned about.

What makes more sense?

Fixing the problem so it will not break again or applying a workaround that will cause another outage?

Arguing the point to take that bit longer to fix the underlying issue is far better than explaining why the live environment went down again.

Do Not Forget Your Retrospective

The ultimate goal of troubleshooting is to find the root of a problem. The secondary goal though should be to never have it happen again. For this, having a discussion with all involved and planning how to avoid the issue is crucial.

Document the issue and how the problem was resolved. Having something to refer back to if the problem did somehow ever happen again will save time.

Summary

In this chapter, we explored the following about troubleshooting:

- Learn to understand your problem, by explaining to yourself and "others."

- Break your problem down to the smallest components and work from there.

- The five whys and how simply asking why one thing is broken can help you find the main culprit.

- How to build a theory on what could be causing your problem and proving your theory before applying any solution to your live environment.

- The correct ways to ask for help, including what you should do before you ask for help.

- Things to avoid when troubleshooting.

CHAPTER 12

Advanced Administration

This final chapter of *Linux System Administration for the 2020s* is going to explore ways that you, the Linux sysadmin, can dig deeper into the Linux operating system to find the information you need.

This chapter will start by looking into system analysis and help you understand how to get more information from your Linux system without having to spend hours doing so. We will discuss what tools can be used to both extract and decipher system information for you to get your answers that bit quicker.

When system analysis tools and techniques do not give you all the information you need, the use of additional tools is required to get more. We will spend the remainder of this chapter looking at how you can extract the last drops of information out of your Linux operating system.

System Analysis

As a Linux system administrator, you will have spent time looking through configuration files and general system health to try to pinpoint the source of a user's problem. This process can normally be painful and can take time you do not want to spend. Having the correct tools can go a long way in helping get to the bottom of an issue and allow you to focus on more interesting things.

© Kenneth Hitchcock 2022
K. Hitchcock, *Linux System Administration for the 2020s*,
https://doi.org/10.1007/978-1-4842-7984-7_12

Here are some quick tools you can use to get information about a Linux system.

Tools for the Sysadmin

Maintaining or running a Linux estate can be a simpler job if you have the right tools available and know how to use them in a way that makes sense to you.

Sosreport

With all enterprise Linux systems, "sosreport" is used to extract information for support teams. Sosreport is a plugin-based tool that can be run with different parameters to export different information. Sosreport's output is often requested by enterprise support teams when support cases are raised and is always worth uploading whenever a new support case is raised.

Sosreports are an archive of the problematic system configuration and logs. Support teams are able to use the sosreport to better understand the problems being experienced without requesting different configuration files.

A sosreport can be created without specifying any parameters as follows, but can also have additional parameters passed to cut down the output or increase what is extracted:

```
# sosreport
```

As a Linux sysadmin, you may wish to use sosreports for your own diagnosis queries. Sosreports can be extracted manually if you wish to look into a user's problem from your own test system.

If manual extraction of sosreports does not interest you, there are tools that can be used to extract and summarize the configuration within the reports.

XSOS

One such tool is xsos, developed and maintained by community members; xsos can take sosreport inputs and create a nice summary of the system. For support staff, this saves more time than most realize as there is no need to extract or sift through configuration files for a quick overview.

To run a basic test of xsos, you can run the following command:

```
# curl -Lo ./xsos bit.ly/xsos-direct; chmod +x ./xsos; ./
xsos -ya
```

The preceding command will only output details from the system you are running it from. If you want to view a sosreport output, you will need to install the xsos tool and pass the path to your sosreport.

The basic xsos report will output the following areas:

- Summarized dmidecode output

- Operating system details

- Kdump configuration

- CPU details

- Interrupts and softirq

- Memory

- Storage

- LSPCI

- Network information including firewall

- Kernel tuning configuration

> **Tip**   Automate your Linux systems to automatically generate these reports on a regular basis and upload the output to a central share. If you ever have a major issue, you can refer to these sosreports for clues to what could have gone wrong.

System Information

All the device information about your Linux system can be found in the "/proc" directory. In the "/proc", there are different files like "meminfo" or "cpuinfo" which will show you the relevant information about each component. The "cpuinfo" file, for instance, will show you all the information about all the CPUs attached to your Linux system including CPU flags.

Shortcut Tools

If digging through "/proc" files is not for you, the tools listed in Table 12-1 can also be used to get basic information about your Linux system. Being familiar with these tools will allow you to gain quick access to device information when you need to diagnose any issues quickly.

Table 12-1. *Basic Linux system tools for hardware information*

Linux Command	Description
lshw	Will list a full summary of all hardware recognized by your system
lscpu	Summary of all CPU information, similar to running # cat /proc/cpuinfo
lsblk	Quick list of all storage devices attached
lsusb	List of all USB devices plugged into your Linux system
lspci	Lists all the PCI controllers and devices plugged into PCI slots
lsscsi	Lists all the scsi and sata devices attached to your system

More Details

If the details are not enough in the shortcut tools, you can use the tools listed in Table 12-2 to give you that bit more.

Table 12-2. *Tools for a bit more details*

Linux Command	Description
hdparm	Prints out details like geometry for a storage device
dmidecode	Can be used to give more in-depth information about your systems. Using the "-t" parameter followed by either "memory," "processor," "system," or "bios" will give you more details around each one

System Tracing

Learning what is happening under the covers is what sometimes is needed when you are stuck with a stubborn issue. There are a few tools that can help you as the Linux sysadmin get these lower-level details.

Strace

An extremely useful tool to see what is happening with a process or running application is "strace." Strace can be run as a prefix to a command or application and can also be attached to a running "pid."

Installation

Strace is available in most common repositories in almost all Linux distros. In the case of Fedora, strace can be installed as follows:

```
# dnf install strace -y
```

The following command will show you everything that happens when you run the free command:

```
# strace free -h
```

Output to a File

A very useful thing to do when using strace is to send the output to a file; from there, you can search for strings or values.

To output a strace command to a file, you can run a similar command to the following:

```
# strace -o testfile.txt free -h
```

The output file can then be viewed in a text editor and in some cases may even display different calls in different colors to make interpreting slightly easier.

What to Look For

The following are some useful things to look for with strace:

- Any files trying to be opened but do not exist or showing potential permission denied -13 errors

- Files being written to that have permission issues

- Network traffic from a process or application transmitting over the network

Useful Strace Parameters

Table 12-3 lists some useful parameters you can use with strace.

Table 12-3. *Strace parameters*

Parameter	Description
-p	Allows strace to be attached to a running pid
-c	Creates a summary of all the different system calls that were run for the process
-t	Shows a timestamp of when each line was run
-e trace=open	Filters all system calls to only include open calls. Other options include all, write, signal, abbrev, verbose, raw, and read
-q -e trace=	Allows trace to be set to file, process, memory, network, and signal

Systemtap

Another nice tool to extract information from your Linux system is "systemtap." Systemtap is a scripting language that uses files with the ".stp" extension. Systemtap can be used to diagnose complex performance or functional problems with kernel-based Linux platforms.

Installation

Systemtap can be installed manually or can be installed using the automated installation method.

Manual Install

The basic packages needed for systemtap are systemtap and systemtap-runtime. On a RHEL system, the following command will install your packages:

```
# yum install systemtap systemtap-runtime -y
```

Automated Install

Stap-prep is a simple utility that will work out the requirements for systemtap and install them for you. To use stap-prep, you need to install the package "systemtap-devel".

Once you have installed the systemtap-devel package, run the command stap-prep. The required files for the current running kernel will be installed.

Systemtap Users

If you are using the normal Linux kernel module backend, you can run "stap" as root. However, if you want to allow other users to create and run systemtap scripts, the following users and matching groups must be created:

- stapusr

- stapdev

Any users in "stapdev" and "stapusr" group will be able to run systemtap as if with root privileges. Users in "stapusr" only may launch (with "staprun") precompiled probe modules.

Users in the "stapusr" group may also be permitted to create basic unprivileged systemtap scripts of their own.

Systemtap Scripts

On all systems where systemtap is installed, you will have access to example scripts. These can be found at the following location:

/usr/share/systemtap/examples/

Running Systemtap Scripts

As mentioned, systemtap files are saved with .stp extensions and are run using the stap command.

To test systemtap, use the examples provided like the disktop.stp example script. This script shows what processes are currently writing to disk. The script can be found at

```
/usr/share/systemtap/examples/io/disktop.stp
```

What this script does is probe the kernel for information about the block devices attached:

```
# stap -v /usr/share/systemtap/examples/io/disktop.stp
```

Once the script is running, you will see the script probing the kernel for any disk operations.

To test this, run on a DD command similar to the following in a new window:

```
# dd if=/dev/zero of=file.txt count=1024 bs=1048576
```

Cross Instrumentation

Often in live environments, it may not be possible to install all the systemtap packages to run probes or tests. For this reason, it is possible to create systemtap modules and execute them by only installing the systemtap-runtime package.

This would allow one system to be used as the compiler that can be used to compile the systemtap instrumentation modules. The kernel versions would need to match however, and the systems would need to be the same architecture. To build different modules for different kernel versions, just reboot the build system into a different kernel.

To create a cross-instrumentation iotop module, you can run the command:

```
# stap -p 4 -m iotop /usr/share/systemtap/examples/io/iotop.stp
```

Once created, these modules then need to be copied by a sysadmin to /lib/modules/`uname -r`/systemtap of the system you want to execute the module on.

System Tuning

Another important aspect of Linux system administration is understanding how to tune a Linux system for the task it needs to perform.

This process can be difficult if you have no guidance from any of the vendors or if you are new to managing Linux systems.

Tuned

The process of tuning your Linux system can involve an in-depth understanding of kernel parameters and system configuration. However, there is a very nice tool called "tuned" which has the ability to tune a system using different profiles.

Installation

Tuned can be simply installed with yum on a RHEL system as per the following:

```
# yum install tuned
```

Tuned will also need to have the service enabled and started:

```
# systemctl enable tuned
# systemctl start tuned
```

Using Tuned

Tuned has a number of profiles that are provided with it during the installation. To see the current active profile, you can run the following command:

```
# tuned-adm active
```

To list all available profiles, you can run the command

```
# tuned-adm list
```

Finally, to switch to a different profile, you can run

```
# tuned-adm profile <name of profile>
```

Summary

In this chapter, you were introduced to the following:

- Linux system analysis tools such as sosreports and how to read them in a quick and easy manner

- Standard system tools that can be used to extract system information

- System tracing tools such as strace and systemtap

- System tuning in a simple way using the tuned utility

Index

© Kenneth Hitchcock 2022
K. Hitchcock, *Linux System Administration for the 2020s*,
https://doi.org/10.1007/978-1-4842-7984-7

Printed in the United States
by Baker & Taylor Publisher Services